GUIDANCE MONOGRAPH SERIES

SHELLEY C. STONE

BRUCE SHERTZER

Editors

GUIDANCE MONOGRAPH SERIES

The general purpose of Houghton Mifflin's Guidance Monograph Series is to provide high quality coverage of topics which are of abiding importance in contemporary counseling and guidance practice. In a rapidly expanding field of endeavor, change and innovation are inevitably present. A trend accompanying such growth is greater and greater specialization. Specialization results in an increased demand for materials which reflect current modifications in guidance practice while simultaneously treating the field in greater depth and detail than commonly found in textbooks and brief journal articles.

The list of eminent contributors to this series assures the reader expert treatment of the areas covered. The monographs are designed for consumers with varying familiarity to the counseling and guidance field. The editors believe that the series will be useful to experienced practitioners as well as beginning students. While these groups may use the monographs with somewhat different goals in mind, both will benefit from the treatment given to content areas.

The content areas treated have been selected because of specific criteria. Among them are timeliness, practicality, and persistency of the issues involved. Above all, the editors have attempted to select topics which are of major substantive concern to counseling and guidance personnel.

Shelley C. Stone

Bruce Shertzer

RATIONAL-EMOTIVE THERAPY

KENNETH T. MORRIS
H. MIKE KANITZ

CENTRAL MICHIGAN UNIVERSITY

With a Foreword by
ALBERT ELLIS
INSTITUTE FOR ADVANCED STUDY
IN RATIONAL PSYCHOTHERAPY

HOUGHTON MIFFLIN COMPANY · BOSTON
ATLANTA · DALLAS · GENEVA, ILL. · HOPEWELL, N.J. · PALO ALTO

ISBN: 0–395–200369

Library of Congress Catalog Card
Number: 74–11961

CONTENTS

FOREWORD

Kenneth T. Morris and Mike Kanitz have done an excellent job, in this monograph, of expositing some of the deceptively simple formulations of rational-emotive therapy in highly understandable English. I say deceptively simple because RET, although it has at its foundation one of the most uncomplicated theories of human personality and disturbance — the by now fairly well-known A-B-C theory that I first delineated in 1955 — actually includes a consideration of many psychological and philosophic complexities. Consequently, it is often easily stated but not so easily (or fully!) understood. In fact, as Professors Morris and Kanitz adequately show, it is frequently distinctly misunderstood.

Rational-Emotive Therapy, for all its conciseness, is remarkably inclusive. Naturally, it doesn't include everything that I consider important in RET. I have applied its methods, in quite a number of books, to specific sex, love, and marital problems; in another book, to the problem of murder and assassination; and in still another, to executive leadership. Paul Hauck has applied it to the area of pastoral counseling. Other practitioners and writers have utilized it in various other areas, which are hardly covered (mainly for lack of space) in this book. So the present monograph is hardly encyclopedic.

Nonetheless, Professors Morris and Kanitz have covered, in relatively few pages, the core philosophy and central practices of RET, and I think that they have done so unusually well. It would have been nice if they were highly experienced practitioners of rational-emotive therapy themselves. But as members of the teaching profession in a graduate field of study, counseling and counselor education — which has been largely favorable, for the last three decades, to methods of therapy that are highly nondirective and nonactivist — I think that they are in an excellent position to assay RET more dispassionately and eclectically than dyed-in-the-wool devotees of the system would have been. I am, therefore, delighted that they have been, throughout this monograph, so beautifully openminded and objective. I know that they have worked very hard at presenting both the pros and cons of RET; and again, I think they have done so very well.

As for my personal contacts with Ken and Mike in the course of the workshop in RET that I gave at Western Illinois University at Macomb, and during the lengthy interview they did with me at that time, let me say that I found these contacts both enjoyable and educational. If they obtained some useful material from me, I also learned considerably from meeting with them. I am delighted to have encountered them and to have had the subsequent experience of learning more about them — and myself! — from reading their honest book.

ALBERT ELLIS

Institute for Advanced Study in Rational Psychotherapy
New York City

EDITORS' INTRODUCTION

Since its initial promulgation in the mid-1950s Rational-Emotive Therapy has become increasingly well known and widely used as a psychotherapeutic technique. The degree to which RET has become known and accepted among practitioners of counseling and psychotherapy is due largely to the efforts of its originator, Albert Ellis.

Kenneth Morris and Mike Kanitz present the core of RET in an excellent and unique way. Few authors of a secondary source have had the opportunity for direct contact with the originator of a theory, and fewer still the direct participation of a theorist in the preparation of a manuscript. Dr. Ellis is to be commended for his generous participation in the preparation of the monograph and has enriched it immeasurably by permitting use of his presentation material and a personal interview. Professors Morris and Kanitz clearly went beyond what was required of them to develop and present this unique counseling and therapy approach.

SHELLEY C. STONE
BRUCE SHERTZER

AUTHORS' INTRODUCTION

The authors agreed to write this monograph after Shelley Stone and Bruce Shertzer agreed to let us be different and write our own thing, in our own way. This monograph is the result of our efforts.

We believe the monograph offers a unique organization. It does offer the reader insight into rational-emotive therapy (RET) and the philosophy of its founder, Albert Ellis. We are pleased that we established a personal and professional relationship with Albert Ellis and cannot begin to thank him for his *original* contributions to this volume. His responses to our queries as delineated in Chapter 3 should prove invaluable to the reader. Similarly, his insights into the current issues and future directions of RET, described in Chapter 5, are worth reflection.

We would like to thank others for their contributions to our effort: first, William A. Carlson, for his helpful suggestions; second, Ann Salisbury and Tina Abbey, whose research assistance was deeply appreciated; third, Diane Burgbacher, for burning the midnight oil in her efforts to type the manuscript; and finally, Albert Ellis, for being himself and contributing so selflessly to this monograph.

K. T. M.
H. M. K.

A cognitive-behavior psychotherapy system designed to help humans achieve their basic goals or values, especially:

1. To survive, exist, and remain alive.

2. To be relatively happy.

3. To live successfully within a social group.

4. To experience a meaningful relationship with one or more selected individuals.

5. To work productively and creatively at some kind of remunerative activity.

Background Data

The introductory chapter is designed to expose the reader to the background of Albert Ellis and to the evolution of rational-emotive therapy (RET). The majority of the monograph deals with RET as the creation of Albert Ellis. One does not write about non-directive counseling without attending heavily to Carl Rogers. Nor does one ignore Freud when discussing classical psychoanalysis. Who would write about Gestalt and omit Perls? Such must also be the case for RET. Although there are numerous therapists practicing RET, the majority of the literature comes from Albert Ellis. There-fore, the vast majority of this effort attends to Ellis.

Albert Ellis' Background

Albert Ellis was born in 1913 in Pittsburgh. He has lived most of his life in New York City.

He has indicated that his childhood existence was one of semi-orphanhood (Burton, 1972). He seldom saw his father, who was a traveling salesman and promoter. Very frequently his father was missing from the home environment for weeks or months. As for his mother, Ellis states that she was "quite unequipped to deal ade-quately with either marriage or child-rearing ..." (Burton, 1972,

p. 104). She left Albert and his brother and sister to themselves. Ellis comments on the fact that, due to her lack of overseeing of him, he was allowed (and later appreciated) much autonomy and independence.

Combined with parental neglect was a lengthy list of physical difficulties. At the age of five Ellis almost died from tonsillitis. He then acquired acute nephritis or nephroses.* Ellis states that he was not able to take any active part in the usual childhood games and activities. It is his belief that he developed into a sissy as compared to his athletically-oriented brother.

Ellis showed the first signs of his reliance upon reason and cognition by refusing to be miserable or to allow his home, physical, or social inadequacies to be more than minor inconveniences. He was shy, anxious, retiring, and non-aggressive, especially sexually and socially. Through the application of reason, he developed compensating abilities. Classmates came to him for help. He was brilliant in school. He became a voracious reader. These, and other achievements, led to the development of much false self-esteem. He admits this, by saying that as a child he erroneously based his concept of his worth upon his accomplishments and popularity.

Ellis received a Ph. D. in clinical psychology from Columbia University in 1947. He became a lay analyst as the result of receiving analysis from a training analyst of the Karen Horney group.

It was shortly after he began practicing classical psychoanalysis that RET began its gestation period. It, as is true for most systems, evolved from and through Ellis' client contact and his growing dissatisfaction with the results and efficiency of psychoanalysis. An equally important factor in the RET evolvement, of course, is Ellis himself. He admits to a very high energy level and an abhorrence of laziness and uninvolvement. Classical analysis did not allow him to expend his energy and be involved. Nor did it appear to him to work very well.

Evolution of RET

Ellis became dissatisfied with classical analysis when he realized that his clients appeared merely to *feel* better, not *get* better. He started utilizing different psychoanalytically-oriented therapy techniques and was amazed to discover that his analysands did at least as well, if not better, with this more superficial approach as had been the case when he used orthodox techniques.

Because of his desire to be involved actively with his clients, Ellis slowly introduced "himself" into the sessions. He did this by

* Ellis is also diabetic, but no mention is made as to when he acquired this illness.

being more quickly and directly confrontive, interpretive, and advice-giving. He also began to use his life, his experiences and ideas, and his philosophy and beliefs as to why people are disturbed and dysfunctional *during* the sessions. The gestation period over, a new child, rational-emotive therapy, was preparing to shoulder its way to the top of the therapy theory pile. Not an insignificant contributor to the birth of RET was the fact that Ellis was his own guinea pig. He taught himself RET. He said, "Albert, challenge your social-sexual beliefs. Is it awful if you fail? Is it terrible if someone rejects you sexually or socially?" His answers, of course, were "No!" He began to *believe* that failure and rejection were *not awful.* And, most importantly, he *acted* on these beliefs. He went out and risked. He met failure and rejection and discovered they meant only that he had failed, *not* that he was a failure. Herein was born the RET thesis that cognition *plus* action (homework) equals success.

Ellis first exposed his peers to RET during an address to the American Psychological Association in 1955. His first written treatise appeared in 1956. As could be expected, the furor which RET created was enormous. Ellis admits that most of his fellow professionals, with the exception of Rudolph Dreikurs, were shocked, appalled, and highly negative, (Ellis, 1974a).

If it is true that quality stands the test of time and endures scathing attacks, then there is quality and merit in RET. It has expanded its influence and is now recognized as a system which can and does work; a system which has contributed to the field; a system which future therapists must be aware of, regardless of whether they eventually choose to practice it or merely eclectically borrow from it.

Summary and Synopsis

As is the case for most therapy systems, RET is the brainchild of one man, Albert Ellis. The seed for RET was, it appears, originally planted in the mind of man by Epictetus, when he said: "Men are disturbed not by things, but by the views which they take of them." However, it was Ellis who took the seed and made it grow.

One can readily note that Ellis' childhood environment *contributed* to the evolution of RET. Ellis would deny any causal relationship, but he would probably admit that his childhood existence (the activating event) gave him the opportunity to examine his thoughts (step B) and thereby change his emotions (step C), especially his feelings of non-aggression, inhibition, and shyness.

RET, as a formal therapy system, is now almost twenty years old.

As a propagandized belief system, it is as old as is Ellis. His life is, and will continue to be, a walking advertisement for RET.

For those desirous of such information, the following is a list of many of Ellis' professional and literary contributions.

Biographical Data

Dr. Ellis is a Fellow of the American Psychological Association and has been President of its Division of Consulting Psychology and a Member of its Council of Representatives. He is a Fellow (and Past President) of the Society for the Scientific Study of Sex; and he is a Fellow of the American Association of Marriage and Family Counselors, the American Orthopsychiatric Association, the American Sociological Association, the American Association for Applied Anthropology, and the American Association for the Advancement of Science.

Dr. Ellis has also been Vice-President of the American Academy of Psychotherapists; Chairman of the Marriage Counseling Section of the National American Association of Marriage and Family Counselors, of Psychologists in Private Practice, of the Divisions of Psychotherapy and of Humanistic Psychology of the American Psychological Association, and of the New York Society of Clinical Psychologists. He has been honored by several professional societies, given the Humanist of the Year Award by the American Humanist Association, and the Distinguished Professional Psychologist Award of the Division of Psychotherapy of the American Psychological Association.

Dr. Ellis has served as Associate Editor of the *Journal of Marriage and the Family, The International Journal of Sexology, Existential Psychiatry, The Journal of Contemporary Psychotherapy, The Journal of Sex Research, Rational Living,* and *Voices: The Art and Science of Psychotherapy.* He has published over four hundred papers in psychological, psychiatric, and sociological journals and anthologies. He has authored or edited thirty-four books and monographs, including *Sex Without Guilt; How To Live With A Neurotic; The Art and Science of Love; A Guide to Rational Living; The Encyclopedia of Sexual Behavior; A Guide to Successful Marriage; Reason and Emotion in Psychotherapy; How to Raise an Emotionally Healthy, Happy Child; Is Objectivism a Religion?; Murder and Assassination; Growth Through Reason; Executive Leadership: A Rational Approach; The Sensuous Person: Critique and Corrections;* and *Humanistic Psychotherapy: The Rational Emotive Approach.*

2

Rational-Emotive
Therapy

It is the authors' intention to present the basic concepts of rational-emotive therapy in this chapter. The theory originated through the works of Dr. Albert Ellis and is a radical approach that teaches people how to solve personal problems. The theoretical nature of man is presented along with the therapeutic principles, RET techniques, interview transcripts, practical considerations for professionals, and summary. The reader is introduced to the most common irrational beliefs that man incorporates into self-defeating behavior. While RET theory is often criticized, especially for its active-directive approach, it remains a psychological approach which is tremendously effective in assisting humans to live a more emotionally satisfying life.

Nature of Man

The philosophical notions underlying most counseling theories are based on the inherent tendencies of man. Freud viewed man as determined by his past history while Adler saw man motivated by the future. Such contrasting positions continue to cause theorists to speculate about the intricate nature of man.

Existential philosophers, such as Kierkegaard (1962) maintain that man by virtue of his existence is intrinsically worthwhile regardless of any external evaluations. Rational-emotive theory differs significantly with many of the more traditional theoretical concepts of man. While rational-emotive theory has no great quarrel with man's self-actualizing tendencies as presented by Maslow (1971), it does contend that it is desirable to put definitions in order. Ellis points out that definitions of worth and worthlessness have no empirical formula by which they can be verified scientifically. He cautions:

> If people consider themselves to be 'worthwhile,' they will tend to feel good about their self-evaluation, and perhaps to be happier and more efficient in their doings. But by considering themselves 'worthy' they also bring in the concomitant concept of 'worthlessness,' and run the danger of creating needless pain and inefficiency. [Ellis, 1962b]

The concepts of worth and worthlessness regarding personhood are actively disputed in RET, but their prominence in many other theories is acknowledged and deemed to be out of the empirical realm.

Thus the nature of man, espoused within the rubric of RET, is that he is a cognitive-emotive-behaving creature. Man, by his very nature, is alive and exists. This observable aliveness is neither good nor bad, and it is desirable that no self-evaluation be attached. The philosophical assumptions forwarded in rational-emotive theory are that human beings have human limitations but are truly able to create and direct their own lives. Man has the right to existence and may choose to enjoy and fulfill himself. In essence, the theory maintains that we are important because we are alive, holistic, and almost always free to direct our own lives as we focus upon personal values and experiences.

The conditions by which one is surrounded, along with biological factors, are definitely accepted within the RET framework as partly responsible for emotional disturbance. According to Ellis (1973c):

> Unlike the orthodox psychoanalytic and the classical behavioristic psychologies, rational-emotive therapy squarely places man in the center of the universe and of his own emotional fate and gives him almost full responsibility for choosing to make or not make himself seriously disturbed. Although it weighs biological and early environmental factors quite importantly in the chain of events that lead to human disorganization and disorder, it insists that nonetheless the individual himself can, and usually does, significantly intervene be-

tween his environmental input and his emotionalized output, and that therefore he has an enormous amount of potential control over what he feels and what he does.

The "enormous amount of potential control" alluded to is man's highly organized or specialized thinking ability. According to theory man's reluctance to employ such high-level cognitive qualities will lead to anxiety, hostility, or depression. The rational-emotive view is that man may choose to create emotional disturbance and almost always may choose to make himself undisturbed again.

The inherent character or basic constitution of man, theoretically speaking, is that he indeed does make himself disturbed by a belief system that accepts assumptions about self and others that cannot be validated. These irrational beliefs which man is capable of incorporating into his philosophy of life, can and do create an emotional disturbance of sorts. Whether humans are biologically or sociologically disposed to the illogical thinking process is not within the realm of this offering to prove or disprove. Rational-emotive theory and the corresponding nature of man include his ability to stifle personal growth by invoking unverifiable superstitions and myths into the thinking process. Many such dogmas are prevalent throughout the history of man. Man's capacity to neglect high-level thinking is considered part of his nature. This avoidance allows man to create absolutes which are unsound and incongruous. Man often accepts such unreasonable beliefs, which tend to result in ineffective functioning, e.g., self-deprecation, hostility, depression, etc. Such irrational beliefs allow man to be preoccupied with self-evaluation. Rational-emotive theory indicates that man's natural fallibility is part of his humanness. Evaluating self seems to be inborn, and RET therapists agree that man is demandingly perfectionistic and correspondingly error-prone. Such a psychological trap will cause the human organism to engage in such anomalies as ego esteem, worthlessness, self-esteem, and the like. Man will invariably, possibly without conscious thought, enter into the notions of superiority and inferiority. Inevitably, human beings often seem to strive for enhancement of self at the expense of other humans, and RET views such behavior as irrational. Writers in the field concur that such an avoidance of high-level cognition will create in man the irrational beliefs leading to disturbed behavior. Ellis (1973) adds: "Humans, unfortunately, seem to be almost universally born and reared to give themselves self-evaluation." This would seem to bring into play the comparison of self to others, and again, result in the disturbing ego-play between humans which we all frequently encounter in our personal lives.

With the absence of straight thinking, man is free to create laws to rule the world, when at best, these are only desires, not absolutes.

Ellis (1973) points out that "virtually all human disturbance is the result of magical thinking (of believing in shoulds, oughts, and musts) and can, therefore, be directly and forthrightly eliminated by the individual's sticking rigorously to empirical reality." In reiteration, man tends to avoid high-level thinking by nature, thus, upsetting himself by insisting that (a) "[he] should be outstandingly loved and accomplished, (b) other people should be incredibly fair and giving, and (c) the world should be exceptionally easy and munificent" (Ellis, 1973). At the point where man significantly intervenes and controls what he feels and does, it is apparent that a movement toward self-actualization is underway. If irrational self-rating is absent, if competing for goodness is non-existent, then man is making a growth choice instead of a self-preservation or fear choice. Man is capable of functioning as nothing more or less than the human being he truly is; it is desirable that he accept his own humanity and that of his fellow man. Man has the capacity to maintain emotional well-being by influencing his emotions and behavior and by arriving at self-acceptance through a rational philosophy of life. RET philosophy offers that man will, upon eradicating irrational beliefs, alter his behavior and stop condemning himself. As a result of this, he will also become more responsible to other human beings. The concept of man illustrated above concludes that man has the innate ability to learn how to challenge actively and remove irrational beliefs which support self-defeating behavior. Herein lies a primary tenet relevant to rational-emotive therapy: *it is possible to achieve maximum actualization of human potential through the use of cognitive control of illogical emotional responses.* The theory embraces the assumption that man is capable of both rational and irrational thoughts which are not separated, or different from emotions. The following section will elaborate upon the principles of RET.

Therapeutic Principles

Considering the theoretical nature of humans as both perfectionistic and error-prone; and, given that humans are influenced by language indoctrinations; plus the fact that humans live in neurosis-producing cultures, RET theory suggests that deconditioning and re-education by direct means is an appropriate way of eliminating much of human disturbance. The therapeutic principles of RET certainly do originate through an opposition to other theories. Ellis (1962b) aptly notes:

> . . . still misled by Freudian-oriented theories, I had been stressing psychodynamic rather than philosophic causation, and had been emphasizing what to undo rather than what to unsay and unthink. I had been neglecting (along with virtually all other therapists of the day) the precise, simple declarative and exclamatory sentences which the patients once told themselves in creating their disturbances and which, even more importantly, they were still specifically telling themselves literally every day of the week to maintain these same disturbances.

The elimination of false definitions is paramount if self-damning is to be dealt with in the counseling process. Self-talk, which is redundant and often based upon a false premise, will often lead to irrational thoughts and feelings. When there is no supporting evidence to validate definitions, directive therapy is applied to challenge these corresponding irrational beliefs. The principles of RET are designed to reduce disturbability and not solely to eliminate symptoms. The natural and humanistic approach is to do away with inappropriate disturbance within the human system.

RET is a radical approach that eliminates the deleterious need to "ego trip" while also eliminating the concomitant need to condemn self. Ellis (1971c) states that "RET is also rigorously scientific — meaning that it is based on and consistently uses the principles of empirical validation and logical analysis rather than the principles of magic, mysticism, arbitrary definition, religiosity, and circular thinking." The principles employed in RET are simply stated in terms of A-B-C-D-E, represented as follows:

External Event	A	Activity -or- Action -or- Agent

Self-Verbalizations		Irrational Beliefs Directed at External Event *(A)* -or-
	iB	Inappropriate Beliefs Directed at External Event *(A)* (Cannot be empirically supported)
	rB	Rational Beliefs (Can be empirically supported)

Consequent Affective Emotion	C	Irrational Consequences Inappropriately Ascribed to A -or- Inappropriate Consequences Inappropriately Ascribed to A -or- Rational Consequences Appropriately Ascribed to rB -or- Reasonable Consequences Appropriately Ascribed to rB
Validate or Invalidate Self- Verbalizations	D	Dispute Irrational Beliefs
Change Self- Verbalizations	cE	Cognitive Effect of Disputing iB
Change Behavior	bE	Behavioral Effect of Disputing iB

Irrational Beliefs

The following irrational beliefs are posited by RET to be inherent in man and frequently lead to panic, self-condemnation, and self-doubt, (Ellis, 1973c).

1. The idea that it is a dire necessity for an adult to be loved or approved by virtually every significant person in his community.

2. The idea that one should be thoroughly competent, adequate, and achieving in all possible respects if one is to consider oneself worthwhile.

3. The idea that human unhappiness is externally caused and that people have little or no ability to control their sorrows and disturbances.

4. The idea that one's past history is an all-important determinant of one's present behavior and that because something once strongly affected one's life, it should indefinitely have a similar effect.

5. The idea that there is invariably a right, precise, and perfect solution to human problems and that it is catastrophic if this perfect solution is not found.

6. The idea that if something is or may be dangerous or fearsome, one should be terribly concerned about it and should keep dwelling on the possibility of its occurring.

The following irrational beliefs frequently lead to anger, moralizing, and low frustration tolerance (Ellis, 1973c).

1. The idea that certain people are bad, wicked, or villainous and that they should be severely blamed and punished for their villainy.

2. The idea that it is awful and catastrophic when things are not the way one would very much like them to be.

3. The idea that it is easier to avoid than to face certain life difficulties and self-responsibilities.

4. The idea that one should become quite upset over other people's problems and disturbances.

Theory proposes that a person in need of assistance will invariably be operating at point C or irrational and inappropriate consequences, i.e., depression, hostility, anxiety, etc.

> . . . the individual who feels (at point C) anxious, depressed, ashamed, or hostile when he is rejected by another (at point A) is creating these upsetting feelings by his own highly irrational beliefs at point B. In addition to sane beliefs, he has a number of interlocking insane beliefs, all of which are really tautological and definitional, and are not truly related to reality. [Ellis, 1971c]

Projecting the responsibility for a disturbance or consequence (C) onto the activity, agent, or action (A) is the psychological trap which RET attempts to point out.

> But as long as he devoutly holds on to these irrational beliefs (B), he will strongly tend (1) to feel depressed and/or angry; (2) to be obsessed with his own circular thinking; (3) to mull his thoughts around, sometimes for hours or days on end, in his own inappropriate juices; (4) usually to behave in such a manner that he enhances his chances for

continued rejection; (5) to conclude after a while that he is hopelessly upsettable; and (6) to bring on various other unfortunate symptoms, disturbances, and psychosomatic reactions. [Ellis, 1971c]

An Exemplary Transcript

The following transcript as excerpted from the text *Growth Through Reason* will help the reader to further understand the RET approach to therapy. Dr. Paul A. Hauck is the therapist and Dr. Ellis reacts to the interactions.

. . . .

The client is a twenty-eight-year-old woman who was seen a few times one year prior to the present session because she was somewhat insecure about her impending divorce. At that time, she was able to weather her problems in this connection, and the therapy sessions were therefore terminated. She now returns to therapy in a state of moderate depression, accompanied by episodes of uncontrollable sobbing and anxiety over her depressed state.

First Session

T1: You were saying on the phone that you had a divorce in October and that you have not been depressed until about a week ago.

C2: Well, I'd say about three weeks ago. It's really hard to explain. When we got our divorce, we were still friends and everything. We got along fine. And then when I would see him, like a weekend or something, I was out with another guy and he happened to show up at the same place we were and he sat with us at the table, and we all just had fun together; and when I went home I was depressed. I don't know — my old feelings came back or something. And then the next weekend about the same thing happened; he takes the kids on weekends, and when he brought them home, he stayed for about an hour. We had coffee and talked at the kitchen table, and after he left, I cried and silly things like that; and then by the next Wednesday at the very most, I'd be fine again. And then this week, the thing did not happen on the weekend. I wasn't with him at all. And when he brought the kids home, he did not stay or anything; and I was out with this date for a half hour or so, but I didn't have any of these feelings or anything; but then I was depressed the whole week, and I didn't know why. I didn't feel like I was depressed because of him or anything, but I think I still love him in a way; but I don't want to live with him, and I don't have any desire for him physically or anything. But I feel a certain feeling for him. I care about him. I suppose it is natural after all the years we were married.

T3: Right. How long were you married?

C4: Eight and a half years.

T5: Eight and a half years. And you have how many children?

C6: Three.

T7: It sounds like your first two depressions were the result of kind of feeling a little sorry for yourself because you were lonely.

C8: Right.

T9: You had met him again, and wasn't it too bad that you couldn't make something out of the marriage; and "Gee, we had lovely memories together," and that kind of thing. Is that right?

C10: Right.

T11: But now you are suggesting that the last depression that you had, which has not let up, was due to something else.

C12: I think probably it is. I don't know. I found myself having very little patience with the kids, screaming at them, and then wishing I hadn't. And then at work all day long I sat there and just started crying for no reason. I mean no apparent reason. I just all of a sudden started crying and felt silly about it, but it wasn't something I felt I could control at the time. And I don't know why. I tried to think about it and wonder why I was feeling that way, if I was feeling sorry for myself, if I was lonely, or what it was. There is another situation. I don't like to admit it, but I was seeing a married man, and I think I am in love with him. And he says he loves me and all this stuff; and he says he is going to get a divorce. But he hasn't done it yet, and I think that might have something to do with the depression, too, because I've been seeing him since I got the divorce.

T13: How steadily?

C14: Well, at first it was about twice a week. Well, I see him every day at work, for one thing, but as far as seeing him alone, it was twice or maybe once a week.

T15: For how long?

C16: For six months.

T17: Well, I presume you have a fairly intense relationship going here.

C18: Right.

T19: And you have had intercourse with this man?

C20: Yes.

T21: Okay. Now what happened? Why are you bringing that up now?

C22: Because I think that maybe that had something to do with the depression, because it has been so long that we have been seeing each other, and he hasn't gotten a divorce yet.

T23: Oh, I see.

C24: And I was upset about that, for one thing, because he keeps saying he is going to, and he didn't.

T25: And you were thinking about this about a week ago?

C26: Well, I have been thinking about it for a long time. But I have been just sort of saying to myself — well, he will. And then I think last week I sort of got the idea in my head maybe he's not going to.

T27: I see.

C28: Because it has been — you know.

T29: You began to really, really doubt last week whether he was really sincere.

C30: Yes.

T31: I see. All right. Then what did you tell yourself about that situation when you began to realize that maybe this man is pulling a fast one? Or that he is not really in love with you and has no intentions of divorcing his wife?

C32: What did I think about?

T33: What did you think? What did you say to yourself?

C34: Well, for the past couple months I've been — I keep telling him I'm not going to see him any more until he gets divorced because it's not right, for one thing, and it's not good for me, and it's not good for him and his wife and the kids, and the whole bit. Right? But then I change my mind, and then I ask him to come over or something after I've already said, "I'm not going to see you any more." And so, I don't know what I thought when I start thinking. I really think that he wants to get a divorce, but he doesn't have guts. That's what I think. Maybe I'm kidding myself, I don't know.

T35: You have begun to wonder this past week whether you were in fact kidding yourself. For the first time you really began to seriously think that "maybe I'm being taken for a ride." Before that you were always more positively oriented or persuaded, shall we say? All right. Now you are asking me, I suppose, "Why do I get depressed? Why did I get depressed

last week? What can I do about overcoming this depression?"
Is that what you want to see me about?

C36: Yes, and I think if I had certain goals — you told me once before that I shouldn't wrap myself up so much in one person, which is what I did with my husband. And this I am having a tendency to do again; and I think unless I develop other interests or widen my personality or something, the whole thing is going to happen again. And everybody says, "What do you want? What do you want to do with your life? Do you want a home and family, or do you want to be free?" And I don't know. I'm just kind of — I really don't know what I want. I guess sometimes I feel guilty because sometimes I feel like I'd rather not have the kids. I'd rather be free where I could do just anything I wanted to do. And then I feel guilty because I shouldn't feel this way. And, I don't know — I don't think it's any one thing. It's a combination of things that upsets me.

T37: All right. I think we have to break down what you're doing. In order to control this feeling, we must understand all of the elements that are creating it. You see, actually, from what I hear now, there are probably two ways in which you are depressing yourself. Depression can be caused by one or more of three methods. The first one is to blame yourself for something that you are doing. The second is to pity yourself for something, and the third one is to pity somebody else. For example, if you were to see a child hobbling along with a cane, your heart might want to break over his misery, and you can get pretty depressed over thinking of other people's problems. But you can get obviously just as depressed over thinking of your own problems and how unfair it is, and where you are going, and so on; and I have the feeling that some of the time you are getting depressed because you are looking at your life and you are saying, "What's this all about? Poor me! Here I am not getting anyplace. I waited very faithfully for this man for half a year. I showed him my trust, and the son of a gun isn't coming through the way I hoped he would, and isn't that awful. I feel so sorry for myself because here I am being taken advantage of, and I've been a decent person about this whole thing." Right? Can you sense that that is part of your depression?

C38: Yes, I suppose so.

T39: I don't want you to agree just because I offered it as a suggestion. Do you sense or feel that self-pity is part of your problem?

C40: Yes.

T41: For example, those first two weeks when you were out with your husband, you got depressed after he went home.

C42: Right.

T43: That was self-pity, wasn't it?

C44: Sure.

T45: "Why can't we live together? Wouldn't it have been nice if he had been able to overlook some of my faults?" And this sort of thing. "And he didn't. That's terrible! I ought to feel so sorry for myself because I don't have what I want." Correct?

C46: Yeah.

T47: All right. So probably some of your depression is self-pity. Now I am wondering also whether or not being guilty is part of it — guilty because you are having an affair. Guilty because sometimes you want to reject your children, because they are in the way. I don't know. You fill that in for me. Can you? What do you think you are guilty about?

C48: Well, I think you are right.

T49: About what?

C50: I feel guilty about not wanting the children. Most of the time I don't feel guilty about the affair because I never thought of it in that way. If it was somebody else, I would. I guess I'm like most people. I don't apply the rules to myself. It's wrong for everybody else but it's okay for me.

T51: All right. So then you suspect that you are feeling guilty because of your feelings of not wanting the kids.

C52: Yes.

T53: What do you mean when you say you don't want them? You mean they should be given away? You wish you never had them? You wish they were dead? Or what are you talking about?

C54: I don't know. I don't like the responsibility of the children. If they could just all play together. But you have to discipline them, and you have to teach them; you have to this, and you have to that, and I —

T55: It gets to be a heavy burden. Is that what you mean?

C56: Yes, but then — I mean — nobody made me have them. If I am mature enough to have them, then I should be mature enough to take care of them.

T57: When you notice that sometimes you are not fully the mother that you want to be, then you blame yourself. Is that it? All right, now the question is, are you right for blaming yourself for being an inadequate and disinterested mother?

C58: Well, it can't be anybody else's fault. Nobody else makes me do whatever I do or think whatever I think.

T59: I didn't say fault. I grant you that what is happening there with the children is between you and the children, and therefore most of the things that go wrong might very well be your fault. Correct? I'm saying. "Should you blame yourself because it is your fault?" Do you know what I mean by *blame?* I mean something very precise when I say blame. I mean that you are not only dissatisfied with yourself as a mother, which might be very accurate and correct to say; but you are also dissatisfied with you as a person. In other words, you don't like yourself period. Not only don't you like your mothering, you don't like yourself as a *woman,* who happens to be a mother. You are not just saying that your mothering characteristics are wanting. That would be correct, because right now you don't feel very much like a mother. You've got responsibilities you don't want. It would be very nice to give the kids to someone else until they are ten years old, and then you can come back and take care of them. Right? Okay. So you are right when you say, "I don't think I'm being the greatest mother in the world to these kids." Then you say, "— and that makes me an awful, worthless, good-for-nothing human being." And that — that is when you get depressed. Not when you admit that you are not a good mother. It is when you convince yourself that you are not a good person because you happen not to be a good mother. Follow me?

C60: Yes.

T61: Explain it to me then.

C62: Well, I think what you mean is that — well, like, not everybody could be a good carpenter. You could try and try forever, and you could not be a good carpenter. But it's not your fault that you can't be a good carpenter because you have tried; and the same way, just because I am not a good mother does not mean that I am not a good person. But then there are other things that you are not good at too, so —

T63: Well, now you are saying, of course, that it's okay that you are not a good mother as long as you are good in something else.

C64: Yes.

T65: You've got to be good in a bunch of other stuff. Now, *why* do you have to be? Why can't you be lousy at a lot of things? In other words, I could point out right here that you are probably a lousy bicycle driver, aren't you?

C66: No.

T67: No? Oh, I'm sorry. Okay. Are you a lousy —

C68: Housekeeper.

T69: Okay. You're a lousy housekeeper. You're a lousy housekeeper. You're a lousy mother. You're a lousy — what else?

C70: The things that women are supposed to be.

T71: Most women *are* good at, you mean?

C72: Okay.

T73: Let's not say *supposed to* because that is simply not the way to define it. A lot of women say, "Why? There is no particular reason why I should be good at housekeeping."

C74: Well, this is the way I feel. But then when — well, the majority of people, which you know, which is your society, right?

T75: Right.

C76: When the society you live in demands that you be a good mother and a good housekeeper, it's — hard to keep this attitude. You can't.

T77: I agree it's hard to keep it. But it's harder if you don't. What you have to do is ask yourself whether society and all your friends are really correct. Are you a worthless person because you're not a good mother and a good housekeeper and have a few other failings along with those? Does that mean you are not a good person? Does that mean you have no value any more, at least to you? Now maybe in order to be valuable to these other people and friends of yours, maybe you have to be a good mother because that is the only kind of people they will respect. See? Okay. But does that mean just because you don't have their respect that you can't have your own respect? That is what has happened. You see when you get depressed the way you do, you are saying, "I can't respect myself any more and like myself. I am not important to *me* any more because I am not important to *them*, because I don't fulfill the expectations *they* want out of me." Now that is when you get depressed, when you think you are not important to yourself any more. If you said to yourself, "Well, I am still very important to me. I am a wonderful person. Now, that's not enough to make friends with those people. I am afraid they are going to reject me because in order for me to be friends with them I have to be a good mother, too. However, all right, so I'll have to put up with that. So I'm not going to have their friendship.

See? That's just too bad." Would you be depressed then? If you had your own self-respect and still weren't a good mother and did not have their friendship, would you be depressed? Would you feel guilty?

Dr. Ellis' Reaction

Dr. Hauck zeros in on the essence of the client's problem of depression: not the activating events (point A), her boyfriend's failure to divorce his wife and marry her, and her disinterest in her children, but her irrational belief system (point B). She is clearly telling herself that she *should* be married after a six-month affair, and that she is *supposed to* be a good mother; and that consequently it is *awful* when she is not yet remarried and when she does not want to take the responsibility for her children. He points out that she might possibly accept herself as a person, despite her poor mothering, if she were only good at other things. But why he asks (at least by implication), does she have to be good at *anything* in order to accept herself?

He finishes up this part of the session, however, with an inelegant solution: that she could convince herself, "Well, I am still very important to me. I am a wonderful person. I happen to be a rotten mother — that's true — but I am a wonderful human being." For practical purposes, this solution is all right since she can hold that she is a wonderful person merely because she exists, in spite of her failings. But philosophically, she has no more reason for calling herself a "wonderful person" than she has for calling herself a "bad person." Both designations are definitional or tautological and cannot really be empirically proven.

More elegantly, the therapist could try to get her to accept the fact that she is a person who does both good and bad *deeds* but that she does not have to rate her *self* at all. Instead of trying to help her gain *self-respect* — which is still a rating of herself — he could try to help her gain *self-acceptance,* which is a more objective term denoting that she exists, that she has both fortunate and unfortunate traits, and that she can still choose to focus on enjoying herself even if she always has poor traits and even if (in an extreme case) these traits far outweigh her good ones. *Self-acceptance* (or *self-choosing*) implies that she chooses to stay alive and seek joy (and avoid pain) but *not* to rate herself, (Ellis, 1971c).[1]

. . . .

[1] Reprinted from *Growth Through Reason* with permission of Albert Ellis and the Institute for Advanced Study in Rational Psychotherapy.

Authors' Comments

For those who imply that RET therapists impose values, it is interesting to note that Dr. Hauck very clearly enters into a validation process at T39 when he encourages the client not to accept his hypothesis unless it is correct. He then elaborates upon the original hypothesis to allow the client to respond again, C40, C42, and again, C44, C46, and C48, affirmatively. The validating experience is repeated again in T61 as Dr. Hauck requests that the client explain what had previously been stated by the therapist for which the reply was affirmative. It seems indicative in this case, that the therapist has some mastery in hypothesis testing in a very humanistic manner.

While RET theory has risen to prominence in the last decade, Ellis often credits certain origins to the ancient philosophers, especially Epictetus, when pointing out that internalized sentences at B tend to scramble perceptions and attitudes toward A, external agents, actions, or activities. To combat irrational beliefs the rational-emotive therapist employs an active-directive technique. Ellis (1971c) calls this a "Socratic-type dialogue through which the client is calmly, logically, forcefully taught that he'd better stop telling himself nonsense, accept reality, desist from condemning himself and others, and actively persist at making himself as happy as he can be in a world that is far from ideal." Parenthetically, the reader is encouraged to read the last chapter of *Reason and Emotion in Psychotherapy*, which elaborates upon many of the natural grandiose tendencies man displays in an apparent attempt to deny his very humanity, the fallibility he exhibits in a quest for perfection. Laughridge (1972) finds that:

> Clients who tend to rate their selves on the basis of their past performances, or who condemn their total worth on the basis of a bad performance, are particularly resistant to listening to, let alone accepting, interpretations of their irrational thinking. Since these individuals construe practically everything in self-downing terms, they are likely to feel threatened by an interpretation of their behavior even in a therapeutic setting: they may twist or distort the therapist's explanation or interpretation of how they are creating their own negative emotions into a statement of personal condemnation.

The authors concur from personal experience that "twisting or distorting" explanations or interpretations does exist in therapy, and also such behavior often indicates a resistance to change. Facilitating the reorganization of irrational beliefs is not an easy task, nor is it a simple matter to put into words. It is apparent that many non-directive therapists are aghast at active-directive techniques. This undoubtedly comes about due to the fact that any form of didactics or manipulation has a negative connotation. Many passive therapists have never struggled with the notion that feeling better does not necessarily lead to getting better. Ellis (1972c) comments on today's popular approaches to help people feel better during therapy:

> Perhaps the most human thing about a human being, moreover, is his ability to symbolize, to think, and to talk to himself; indeed, the one thing which he is able to do which probably no other creature on earth can do is to think about his thinking — to question and challenge his own hypotheses about himself and the world. Thinking about thinking, moreover, can be unusually pleasurable, creative, and constructive. Consequently, when a therapeutic procedure over-emphasizes getting the individual to feel deeply and to honestly express his feelings it tends in some ways to help him dehumanize himself, to surrender his problem-solving abilities, and to forego some of his greatest satisfactions. In this sense, such a procedure may actually be anti-therapeutic.

It logically follows that feeling "good" is generated by the human being internalizing sentences that will make him/her feel better. Concomitantly, feeling "bad" is just around the corner. Thus, feeling better *and* getting better are the goals of RET. The principles which are directly and actively applied in rational-emotive therapy are incorporated in the A-B-C-D-E re-education procedures. The following section includes RET techniques, and the principles will be more vividly understood by the reader through the explanation of various approaches.

RET Techniques

Many rational-emotive techniques are employed by therapists to eliminate self-defeating behaviors. Individual therapists or counselors vary in techniques applied to situational experiences. The one primary principle, which Ellis alludes to as the missing "vector" in other therapies (Ellis, 1974b) is homework. That is, the notion of individual homework is almost always applied no matter what procedure or technique is involved in therapy. Whether it is an individual session or a group session, the homework assignment is important and suggested by most RET proponents. Basically, the rationale is to have the person actively dispute illogical premises which lead to irrational beliefs. The Education Research Group (1967) offers a theoretical Law of Mental Declension to explain that the mind is naturally lazy. It is suggested that not disputing irrational beliefs is a form of mental loafing. The Law draws an analogy from thermodynamics and claims a similar psychological rule in which the level of consciousness rises and falls depending upon the level of attention and involvement. Thus, cognitive processes are believed to exist often in some involuntary state lower than the threshold of awareness. One only need read a "Weekend of Rational Encounter" (Ellis, 1969d) to find concentrated experiencing of the highest level. The added ingredient in such a therapeutic experience is the teaching of personality skill refinement in and out of the therapy session.

Homework

The requirement of homework is stressed so that one can more easily come in contact with one's irrational beliefs through higher-level cognition. Any shaming or condemning exercise will almost immediately provide an opportunity to actively dispute irrational thoughts and feelings which lack validation. May (1969), confronting the daimonic world of illness, will more clearly demonstrate the phenomenon.

> Not that the rational information about the disease is unimportant; but the rational data given to me add up to something more significant than the information itself. The names are symbols of a certain attitude I must take toward this daimonic situation of illness; the disorder expresses a myth (a total pattern of life) which communicates to me a way in which I must now orient and order my life. This is so whether it is for two weeks with a cold or twelve years with tuberculosis; the quantity of time is not the point. It is a quality of life. In short, the image by which I identify myself changes by its contact with the myth portraying the daimonic in the natural processes of disease.

It is suggested that undisputed belief systems which maintain certain irrational ideas are in the realm of the daimonic. Such philosophies of life create inappropriate emotions which have the power to envelope the whole person. Homework allows one to release any total dependency on some deitizing therapist, and at the same time, to dispute the daimonic myths that one tends to integrate into self-defeating behavior. No homework requirements are given which suggest inappropriate self-revelation, which Jourard (1968) says may be idolatrous or suicidal in certain situations. The fact remains that responsibly planned homework will create a responsible attack upon guilt, self-downing, blaming, resentment of others, and almost all self-defeating behaviors. The authors forward the assumption that once one internalizes the A-B-C-D-E principles of RET, and engages in relevant homework assignments, everyday life situations will soon replace such assignments and will invoke practice at living a more rational life while eliminating beliefs which cannot be validated.

Tosi (1974) presents six stages of counseling identified by Quaranta which include awareness, exploration, commitment, skill development, skill refinement, and change or redirection. The skill development stage alludes to practice in real-life situations. These stages of the counseling process may be an efficient way for both the helper and helpee to conceptualize personal progress within the rational-emotive process. More importantly the stages might be incorporated into an educational procedure which allows one to view self-in-situation. Being given the opportunity to evaluate one's progress and not one's self is a primary goal in rational-emotive therapy. With some elaboration, the stages might be incorporated into a form for homework which would measure therapeutic progress in a humanistic-scientific manner.

A Homework Report has been developed for use in real-life settings (Table 1). It brings together the A-B-C-D-E comprehensive procedure which is a highly active-cognitive approach. The emphasis on the homework report encourages one to actively deal with the effects of undesirable emotional feelings, actions, or habits. Also, irrational philosophies and ideas are identified and dealt with actively if one chooses to make a commitment to work. The action (A), belief (B), and consequences (C) are presented and may be disputed (D). The cognitive effect (E) may be listed if new behavior follows change in cognition. Such assignments outside of the therapy or counseling sessions also adhere to another tenet of rational-emotive theory, namely, discipline. Discipline is indeed paramount in any attempt to change basic personality patterns. If one has been both negatively and positively rating self for years, a form of training which develops the self-control that ultimately leads to living efficiently is required. Such discipline never seeks to punish, but instead, attempts to correct self-condemnation. Eliminating self-damning is desirable for the acceptance of human fallibility in self and others.

Other Methods

Ellis (1973c) is emphatic about RET employing a wide variety of methods including behavioristic desensitizing and operant conditioning procedures, didactic teaching, bibliotherapy procedures, philosophic discussions, reality testing, and other re-educational

TABLE 1

Homework Report

Consultation Center

Institute for Advanced Study in Rational Psychotherapy

45 East 65th Street, New York, N.Y. 10021 / (212) LEhigh 5-0822

Name .... Date .... Therapist ....

Instructions: Please draw a circle around the number in front of those feelings listed in the first column that troubled you *most* during the period since your last therapy session. Then, in the *second* column, indicate the amount of work you did on each circled item; and, in the *third* column, the results of the work you did.

	Amount of Work Done				Results of Work		
Undesirable Emotional Feelings	**Much**	**Some**	**Little or none**		**Good**	**Fair**	**Poor**
1a Anger or great irritability	1b	....	....	1c	....	....	....
2a Anxiety, severe worry, or fear	2b	....	....	2c	....	....	....
3a Boredom or dullness	3b	....	....	3c	....	....	....
4a Failure to achieve	4b	....	....	4c	....	....	....
5a Frustration	5b	....	....	5c	....	....	....
6a Guilt or self-condemnation	6b	....	....	6c	....	....	....
7a Hopelessness or depression	7b	....	....	7c	....	....	....
8a Great loneliness	8b	....	....	8c	....	....	....
9a Helplessness	9b	....	....	9c	....	....	....
10a Self-pity	10b	....	....	10c	....	....	....
11a Uncontrollability	11b	....	....	11c	....	....	....
12a Worthlessness or inferiority	12b	....	....	12c	....	....	....
13a Other (specify)	13b	....	....	13c	....	....	....
....							

Undesirable Actions or Habits

		b	c
14a	Avoiding responsibility	14b	14c ....
15a	Acting unfairly to others	15b	15c ....
16a	Being late to appointments	16b	16c ....
17a	Being undisciplined	17b	17c ....
18a	Demanding attention	18b	18c ....
19a	Physically attacking others	19b	19c ....
20a	Putting off important things	20b	20c ....
21a	Telling people off harshly	21b	21c ....
22a	Whining or crying	22b	22c ....
23a	Withdrawing from activity	23b	23c ....
24a	Overdrinking of alcohol	24b	24c ....
25a	Overeating	25b	25c ....
26a	Oversleeping	26b	26c ....
27a	Undersleeping	27b	27c ....
28a	Oversmoking	28b	28c ....
29a	Taking too many drugs or pills	29b	29c ....
30a	Other (specify)	30b	30c ....

Irrational Ideas or Philosophies

		b	c
31a	People must love or approve of me	31b	31c ....
32a	Making mistakes is terrible	32b	32c ....
33a	People should be condemned for their wrongdoings	33b	33c ....
34a	It's terrible when things go wrong	34b	34c ....
35a	My emotions can't be controlled	35b	35c ....
36a	Threatening situations have to keep me terribly worried	36b	36c ....
37a	Self-discipline is too hard to achieve	37b	37c ....
38a	Bad effects of my childhood still have to control my life	38b	38c ....
39a	I can't stand the way certain people act	39b	39c ....
40a	Other (specify)	40b	40c ....

(please complete other side)

TABLE 1

Homework Report (continued from previous page)

PLEASE PRINT! BE BRIEF AND LEGIBLE! ANSWER QUESTION C FIRST; THEN ANSWER THE OTHER QUESTIONS.

A. ACTIVATING EVENT you recently experienced about which you became upset or disturbed. (Examples: *"I went for a job interview." "My mate screamed at me."*) ....

rB. Rational BELIEF or idea you had about this Activating Event. (Examples: *"It would be unfortunate if I were rejected for the job." "How annoying to have my mate scream at me!"*) ....

iB. Irrational BELIEF or idea you had about this Activating Event. (Examples: *"It would be catastrophic if I were rejected for the job; I would be pretty worthless as a person." "I can't stand my mate's screaming; she is horrible for screaming at me!"*) ....

C. CONSEQUENCES of your irrational BELIEF (iB) about the Activating Event listed in Question A. State here the one most disturbing emotion, behavior, or CONSEQUENCE you experienced recently. (Examples: *"I was anxious." "I was hostile." "I had stomach pains."*) ....

D. DISPUTING, questioning, or challenging you can use to change your irrational BELIEF (iB). (Examples: *"Why would it be catastrophic and how would I become a worthless person if I were rejected for the job?" "Why can't I stand my mate's screaming and why is she horrible for screaming at me?"*) ....

cE. Cognitive EFFECT or answer you obtained from DISPUTING your irrational BELIEF (iB). Examples: *"It would not be catastrophic, but merely unfortunate, if I were rejected for the job; my giving a poor interview would not make me a worthless person." "Although I'll never like my mate's screaming, I can stand it; he or she is not horrible but merely a fallible person for screaming."*) ....

bE. Behavioral EFFECT or result of your DISPUTING your irrational BELIEF (iB). (Examples: *"I felt less anxious." "I felt less hostile to my mate." "My stomach pains vanished."*)

F. If you did not challenge your irrational BELIEF (iB), why did you not?
....

G. Activities you would most like to *stop* that you are now doing.
....

H. Activities you would most like to *start* that you are not doing.
....

I. Emotions and ideas you would most like to change
....

J. Specific homework assignment(s) given you by your therapist, your group, or yourself
....

K. What did you actually do to carry out the assignment(s)?
....

L. Check the item which describes how much you have worked at your last homework assignment(s): ....(a) almost
every day .... (b) several times a week .... (c) occasionally .... (d) hardly ever.

M. How many times in the past week have you specifically worked at changing and DISPUTING your irrational BELIEFS
(iBs)?
....

N. What other things have you specifically done to change your irrational BELIEFS and your disturbed emotional CONSE-
QUENCES?
....

O. Check the item which describes how much reading you have recently done of the material on rational-emotive therapy:
.... (a) a considerable amount .... (b) a moderate amount .... (c) little or none.

P. Things you would now like to discuss most with your therapist or group
....

(Reprinted by permission)

methods which could be adapted to the rational-cognitive approach.

Tosi (1974) has listed several techniques in rational-emotive counseling: (1) rational-emotive modeling (rem), (2) the PRE-MACK principle of reinforcement, (3) rational-emotive-assertive-training (reat), (4) new cognitive control techniques, (5) rational-emotive imagery, (6) systematic written homework, (7) systematic desensitization and relaxation training (rec), (8) tape listening, and (9) rational-emotive counseling in groups.

The authors choose to elucidate on three particular procedures; Bibliotherapy, Rational-Emotive Imagery, and the Technique for DESensitizing Irrational BELiefS (DESIBELS).

Bibliotherapy

Although various readings may be assigned, *A Guide to Rational Living* (Ellis and Harper, 1961a) is most often cited in the literature as an excellent source for bibliotherapy. The client is asked to read the text to obtain a more thorough understanding of how one might think oneself out of emotional disturbances. Bibliotherapy does help the client to understand that certain tasks can be accomplished outside of the therapy session, and that it is possible to challenge and dispute illogical beliefs which cause inefficient behavior patterns. Also, the more poignant illogical ideas or beliefs are illustrated in *A Guide to Rational Living* through the method of dialogue writing, which introduces the reader to real persons caught in their absolutes (oughts, shoulds, musts), and other perfectionistic godlike requirements for life. Recently asked the question, "When the person learns to evaluate his behavior and not his 'self,' will he automatically improve, or do you give him things to do?" Ellis (1974b) answered "We follow the educational model as opposed to the psychodynamic or medical model. Therefore, we have several things we could use. Everyone of my clients is encouraged to do bibliotherapy. For example, they will read *A Guide to Rational Living.*" The authors in their own way are most interested in presenting this book in that conceptual scheme, namely, suggestions for RET as an educational model.

Rational-Emotive Imagery

Rational-emotive imagery (REI) is a promising behavior-modifying technique used to impress upon the client that a simple change in cognition will allow one to change feelings. In answer to a question from the audience, "How do you deal with a person in a crisis situation, where feelings overcome cognition?" Ellis (1974b) answered, "I don't agree. Their cognitions are really very strong. Their cognitions drove them to where they are, for example, trying suicide. I show them strongly, vehemently, and forcefully that they cognitively created their affective state. I interrupt them and interrupt them and interrupt them until they see it."

Ellis obviously believes that the active-directive treatment is a most efficient way of assisting the person to challenge highly irrational philosophic assumptions. Imagery allows the individual actually to feel some internal change as they think of some absolute necessity; place their shoulds, oughts, or musts on that particular agent, activity, or action; and then change their absolutes to mere desires by changing their sentences (cognitions) to themselves. Imagery simply allows you to challenge or dispute irrational beliefs and feel the change immediately; you are what you eat, so to speak. The authors know that imagery will not work with all people, but it is a powerful technique for those who voluntarily enter into it assisted by a therapist. Maultsby (1971a) explains that the mental self-teaching procedure is based upon the hypothesis that the emotional consequences of imaginary stimuli or real stimuli are relatively the same. By disputing the irrational belief, the person changes the feeling by changing the cognition.

Rational emotive imagery requires the client to think of some anxiety-producing situation or person and then to dispute the irrational belief that others, or the environment, cause such anxiety. This will tend to help eliminate the painful anxiety by admitting one is responsible for the illogical thinking which usually consists of self-deprecating cognitions. The therapist will then assist the client to become aware of which particular irrational beliefs are operational and suggest challenging such illogical premises to do away with painful feelings.

DESIBELS

The Technique for DESensitizing Irrational BELiefS (DESIBELS) was developed by Albert Ellis and used at the Institute for Advanced Study in Rational Psychotherapy in New York City. The technique questions and challenges irrational beliefs. Any of the client's dogmatic beliefs which are rarely questioned may be inserted into the DESIBELS inquiry technique. The technique allows one to quickly tune into a disturbance one is creating in oneself, while eliminating the consequent feelings. Seven basic inquiries are presented:

1. What important irrational belief do I want to desensitize or reduce?

2. What are my specific unreasonable or unrealistic demands connected with this irrational belief?
3. Are these beliefs or demands true?
4. What is the evidence that they are not true?
5. What is the evidence that my main irrational belief is true?
6. What are the worst things that could *actually* happen to me (and not that I could foolishly *make* happen) if my irrational beliefs and unreasonable demands were not fulfilled?
7. What good things might actually happen if my irrational beliefs and unreasonable demands were not fulfilled?

Immediately following each question, illustrative answers to each may be elaborated upon. The requirements are that one spend ten minutes daily asking oneself the seven questions and either writing down the answers or taping answers on a recorder. Operant conditioning or self-management methods are suggested to assist one to use the time daily. The selection of some enjoyable activity is used as a reinforcer which may be indulged in, the day after one has employed the DESIBELS ten-minute technique. One may choose to penalize oneself by engaging in some unpleasant task every day one does *not* use the DESIBELS technique for at least ten minutes. Those who would rather not penalize themselves might enlist the aid of some colleague or associate to see that the penalty is carried out. While it is not necessary that one use operant conditioning with DESIBELS, it is considered more desirable by Ellis if it is used in conjunction with reinforcements and penalties.

Practical Considerations for Professionals

The authors are tempted to list multiple reasons why rational-emotive theory might better be employed in the various helping professions. Also, the inclination is ever present to point out exactly where social workers, counselors, rehabilitation people, employment counselors, and the like, would be more effective in an active-directive approach. We could elaborate upon the possibilities of incorporating RET into the schools, higher education, or adult education. We could explore the underlying psychological constructs of human behavior and the various differences within each framework. Rather, we choose to see RET adopted by the individual professional who sees the efficacy of the theory as relevant to his/her own life. That is, if RET works for the professional therapist or counselor, it will probably work for those he/she comes in contact with. If one applies RET to one's personal life and becomes more tolerant of self and others; if one eliminates grandiose or debilitating rating of self and others; if one discontinues making laws of the universe by invoking absolutes, (shoulds, oughts, musts, necessities); and, if one truly accepts fallible humanity in self and others, it is conceivable that one is well on his way to accepting RET and being willing to engage more actively in cognitive-directive interactions with clients.

The authors point out that the professional who will not give up rating self and others as worthy and unworthy; and will not give up seeking love in building a relationship with a client; and will not give up "being responsible for" vs. "responsible to" others, will often consider the theory too abrasive. To adopt such a theory, one would better be direct, forceful, willing to fail in one's hypothesis and offer another, interrupt, disagree, accept all humans (but not their behavior), and generally be comfortable with other authoritative (not authoritarian) positions.

The main consideration for practitioners is to question the notion that feeling better is equivalent to getting better. The professional might ask the question, "Do my clients improve markedly *away* from the therapy or counseling session?" If the answer comes up "no," we make the calculated guess that a certain amount of deitizing dependency is a possibility and that anti-therapeutic dynamics may be manifested by the lack of noticeable outside behavioral improvement.

RET is a considerably different approach than most therapies. Therefore, the primary considerations for the professional may be; (1) is RET effective in permanently reducing anxiety and hostility, and (2) are the false and irrational philosophic assumptions pointed out by RET actually behind much of inefficient human behavior? With the answers to such questions, the professional is in a position to make decisions relevant to his own personal and professional development.

The limitations of RET are basically the same as those related to other forms of therapy. Those people who do not have the ability to help themselves (serious mental deficiencies, extreme psychotic disorders, the very old and the very young, etc.) do not seem to utilize their own ability to grow and experience (Ellis, 1973c). The brighter the client, the more effective the results of therapy. That is not to say that RET cannot be used with mentally retarded, alcoholics, or drug addicts. On the contrary, RET has been used with good results with others for whom most forms of psychotherapy effect poor rates of improvement (Ellis, 1973c).

Summary and Synopsis

The authors have attempted to present within Chapter 2 the philosophic nature of man put forth by rational-emotive theory. Therapeutic principles and techniques were elaborated upon so as to introduce some of the contrasting elements which differ quite markedly from other theories. The authors attempted to provide an explanation of the RET framework which indicated that human beings are creative individuals who often distort their thinking ability. We attempted to assert that humans are more often philosophically disturbed than they are psychiatrically upset. The transcript of an actual therapy session was included to further clarify that the basic cause of human emotion is human thinking.

Practical considerations for professionals alluded to the specific method. The authors suggest that professionals might first prove the efficacy of such a theory within their personal lives. Only then will such a theory be empirically proven to enhance the quality of life. Limitations are briefly listed but are not much different from those listed within most theoretical frameworks. Citations are provided for those readers who would like to gain an in-depth understanding of RET and its origins. The bibliography will assist those who desire to research further this systematic approach to increase skill in reasoning to meet the stress of modern day man.

3

Reactions to RET

The purposes of this chapter are to: 1) list and discuss some of the positive reactions found in the literature concerning the theory, philosophy, techniques and hypotheses of rational-emotive therapy; 2) list and discuss a majority of the negative reactions discovered by the authors concerning Ellis and RET; 3) present Ellis' reactions to the negative comments as obtained during an interview with him; 4) to present Ellis' responses to questions about RET; and 5) to summarize and synopsize the reactions.

Positive Reactions

Most of the literature available on RET is written and/or contributed to by Ellis. He has frequently written chapters in edited books delineating the principles of RET. All too frequently, the books' editors or authors fail to comment on the RET chapter (Burton, 1969; Harper, 1959; Jurjevich, 1973). Such non-reactionism is also found in most of the counseling and psychotherapy theory books written which discuss RET. When reactions to RET are discovered, they tend to be primarily negative, skeptical, or, at best, neutral (Arbuckle, 1967; Patterson 1966; Wolberg, 1967). In spite of the prevalence of these conditions, the authors were able to discover the following favorable reactions.

1. RET does not portend to be effective with all types of clientele.

Comment: Ellis does admit that RET will probably be less efficient and effective with the following clients: a) persons who are unwilling to accept the hard work and discipline RET requires; b) persons who refuse to think for themselves and need or demand the therapist's guidance; c) persons who dogmatically insist on adhering to some absolutist, religionistic creed; d) persons who are seriously lacking in intelligence and cognitive thinking ability; e) manic-depressives in the manic state; f) catatonics in catatonic withdrawal; g) the very young, usually eight years of age or less and the very old, as both groups are seen as either overly impressionable or overly rigid and inflexible; h) the organically defective; i) clients who insist that their parents and/or backgrounds *caused* their problems and that they *must,* a la the Freudians, track down their traumas; j) autistic children; k) overly agitated schizophrenics; and l) orthodox or overly religious individuals.

2. The irrational and illogical ideas, beliefs, and values which RET delineates as prevalent in Western man do seem to be present in most disturbed and dysfunctional clients.

Comment: Ellis has over 300 research studies which, he says, tend to support this statement. A bibliography listing these studies is currently being written and should be available after this monograph appears. The authors, as practicing therapists, tend to believe that this statement is true. The vast majority of our clients "should" themselves to death. We have no reason to believe other therapists' clients are significantly different from ours.

3. RET has aided the field of psychotherapy in furthering its understanding of the relation between feeling (emotion) and thinking (cognition).

Comment: It is believed by many professionals that RET's greatest contribution has been that of dispelling the Freudian myth that feelings exist apart from thought and are untreatable at a cognitive level. Ellis' belief that you think yourself into your feelings and can, therefore, think yourself out of them drew harsh, if not illogical and irrational, criticisms when it first appeared. However, this tenet is now one of the bases of many therapy systems, especially the directive, behavioral, and cognitively oriented ones which are so prevalent today. Ellis is probably correct in his hypothesis that feelings do not occur *magically*. They are almost always the result of the step B thought processes.

This contribution of RET is given further credence when one considers the fact that there is no evidence to support, or schemata which exists to show, how repressed, unexpressed feelings can exist or influence one's behavior. It would seem that helping the unconscious or preconscious become conscious is nothing more than verbalizing one's unexpressed *thoughts* and *ideas, not* one's unexpressed feelings.

4. Although RET stresses cognition, it does not, as many believe, neglect the emotions.

Comment: Ellis' response to the charge that feelings and emotions are neglected appears later in this chapter. However, the authors do wish to stress the fact that the client's C response, which is affective, feeling, and emotional is almost always the starting point of RET. How then, can anyone seriously purport that emotions are unimportant and/or neglected by the RET therapist?

5. RET admits that the essence of efficient therapy is the changing of attitudes and irrational value beliefs.

Comment: Most therapies are in agreement with this statement. The difference is in the method of achieving attitude change. Ellis addresses himself to this later in this chapter.

Negative Reactions

As was mentioned earlier in this chapter, most critiques of Ellis and RET are heavily negative. An RET practitioner, in perusing the following comments, might contend that they stem from the critics' irrational step B sentences — sentences such as: "Wouldn't it be awful if Ellis were right. He must not be right. If he is, I will have to change my therapy values and beliefs. That would prove how stupid I am. He can't do that to me." The authors are unwilling to support such a reaction wholeheartedly, although it is tempting. We would, however, ask that the reader consider how many of the criticisms are valid, stemming from rational and logical internalized sentences, as opposed to how many may be projections of the critics' doubts about their own therapeutic values, beliefs, and principles.

Each reaction is listed, followed by Ellis' reaction to them, (Ellis, 1974a). The first eight were drawn from Arbuckle (1967) and the next eleven from Patterson (1966). Ellis' responses to these nineteen assertions were taped during an interview with him and are presented verbatim:

1. Ellis confuses assumption with fact. His belief that Man is born with tendencies to behave in certain ways, many of which are illogical, irrational, dysfunctional, and self-defeating is questionable.

Ellis: There are volumes of evidence and data available, along with books such as Walter Pitkin's *History of Human Stupidity,* which prove that there is no society, nor has there ever been, where people are merely straight thinking, undevoted to some superstition, some grandiosity, some religiosity, etc. Zero! Try to find even a single human being who is a truly straight thinker.

Let me give you two examples. How many doctors, who are intelligent and very knowledgeable about health and hygiene, obey the rules? How many don't smoke, don't overeat, get plenty of rest, and so on? Well under 10%. How many college undergraduates, again a bright, well-educated population, procrastinate? Well over 95%. I doubt whether the environment caused these people to behave that way. In every civilization, there are few exceptions.

Reason and Emotion in Psychotherapy presents about thirty-five reasons why people are nutty, illogical and irrational.

RET also, however, believes that humans do have self-actualizing trends. We agree with Rogers, Maslow, Allport and others like them that people have an innate tendency to love, to seek warmth, to care for others, to self-actualize, and so forth. It is humorous that if I tell you people have self-defeating behavior, you will often say: "Prove it. What about the environment?" But you wouldn't ask Maslow to prove his point. Asking such a question proves how prejudiced, intolerant, and biased we often really are.[1]

2. The stress on thinking over feeling is too great. Values are

[1] This response is a paraphrase of Ellis' reply to this question when it was presented at a RET Workshop, February 1 and 2, 1974, at Western Illinois University.

feeling products rather than thinking products. Attempting to think oneself out of them would only suppress the basic feeling.

Ellis: Well, that's his hypothesis, that they're *feeling* products. First of all, he's partly right, because values, as I said at the workshop today, are partly biological. If we didn't have the values of surviving and being happy, etc., we would in all probability die. But that doesn't mean we *must* have them in order to survive; nor, of course, that we *must* survive. But, values are partly biological.

Dr. Arbuckle seems to believe that there's such a thing as feeling divorced from thinking, and there's no evidence for this. In a huge bibliography I'm compiling on RET and cognitive-behavior therapy, I now have about 300 studies, mainly by experimental, social, and clinical psychologists that show that when you change people's thinking, you change their feeling and behavior.[2] Stanley Schacter's studies, for example; those of Richard Lazarus, and all kinds of other controlled studies. So there's no evidence that anybody *purely* feels. Just like there's no evidence that anybody purely senses. You immediately add cognition to sensation. Arbuckle doesn't realize that what he calls *feeling* is a combination of thinking *and* feeling.

Now I may be somewhat misleading if I imply or state, as I may somewhere, that feeling *completely* stems from thinking. If I said that, that would not be so. It stems from feeling, from behaving, and from thinking. But the most important element in human "feeling" seems to be thinking, and, if you change the thinking, you get more profound and lasting emotional modification than if you change anything else.

I think I use words like emotion "largely stems from thinking" or something like that. Arbuckle implies that values are wholly feeling products rather than thinking products. Well, they're neither one nor the other. They're a combination of both. Therefore, if you change your values, you would not suppress your basic feelings. Though, incidentally, you can change a basic feeling. He's got some notion that because your feeling is basic and hedonic, you *have* to be hedonic. Now, you don't. You could be anti-hedonic. Practically nobody is, but you could be. That would be "harmful," but there's no reason you couldn't be self-harming. Arbuckle implies that you

[2] Ellis, A., and Budd, K., *A Bibliography of Articles and Books on Rational-Emotive Therapy and Cognitive Behavior.* In press.

couldn't be anti-hedonic, that hedonism would always come out, that it's inevitable. You could say that to *some* degree; but he implies that you can't change basic feelings at all. And, of course, that's wrong.

We have lots of people who do change basic feelings. Gandhi, for example, was once a run-around, a dandy. Then he changed. The example I usually use is Nathan Leopold, who was a murderer, very anti-social, and then he became a social worker, he married, had a family, and acted very well. So, it is obvious that people can significantly change.

3. Should our feelings be only those which are bright or can we be operational with some feelings which are dark? (e.g., feelings of guilt, depression, remorse, et. al.)

Ellis: I don't know what he means by operational. I'm not clear on that. Operational normally means "clearly defined and stated in testable terms."

Morris: My assumption is that he meant functional.

Ellis: Yes, I think he is really asking, "Is it legitimate to have some feelings which are dark?" Now I think that in *Growth Through Reason,* especially in the introductory chapter, I clearly show that RET is one of the few systems which distinguishes operationally between inappropriate and appropriate feelings.

It's usually good to be "emotional" when you experience some obnoxious stimulus or experience and to feel responsibility, sorrow, regret, annoyance, displeasure, etc. It's good to feel these rather than anxiety, worthlessness, hostility, or guilt (guilt means self-downing). So you'd better have dark feelings.

Now there I would somewhat disagree with some of my associates, who sometimes seem to gloss over negative feelings and think "Well, why should you feel sorry or sad at all?" I don't agree with that. I think you'd better feel sorry, regretful, annoyed, or irritated when at point A, the Activating event or Activating experience, something unpleasant transpires. I have said this in *Growth Through Reason* and in the chapter on RET in Raymond Corsini's *Current Psychotherapies.*

So, feelings better be dark as well as bright, as long as by dark we don't mean magically or absolutistically dark. That's what Arbuckle doesn't see. He doesn't clearly differentiate, as we do in RET, between appropriate and inappropriate dark feelings.

4. If RET teaches that no one is ever to blame for anything, how does one ever develop a sense of self-responsibility?

Ellis: Well, Arbuckle doesn't define blame the way I do. I define blame as: 1) "I did it. I'm responsible." And, 2) self-condemnation, "I am a louse for acting irresponsibly." Today, incidentally, I rarely use "blame," because it is a vague word.

So, if no one ever is to blame in the sense of damning himself, how can he be responsible? Very easily. He says: "I did the wrong thing. I'm going to harm myself and my social group if I keep doing it. Therefore, I'd better (not *have* to) change." While if people condemn *themselves,* their entire being, and not merely their acts, they frequently don't change. They compulsively repeat their self-defeating behavior. And that does little good!

5. With regard to client "insight," RET appears to relegate "experiencing" to an unimportant corner.

Ellis: No. First of all, "insight" is often poor or false. You get false insight under LSD. You think you run the universe or totally understand it. Insight doesn't necessarily mean truth. You "see" something. You feel it. Because you *feel* it, you say it's true for the world at large. But *is* it?

I frequently give my clients the humorous example: Suppose I feel I'm a kangaroo. And you say to me: "Well, *why* are you a kangaroo? *How* are you a kangaroo?" And I reply: "I'm hopping around on the furniture!" Now does that prove I am a kangaroo? The answer is: "Of course not." It proves I *believe,* I *feel* that I am a kangaroo. But that feeling hardly *makes* me one!

Arbuckle doesn't see that experiencing something proves nothing about the outside universe. It only proves that *I* experience it.

I often tell the story that happened twenty years ago. One of my clients was on pot. He was a jazz musician. This was when people didn't take pot very much. And I said: "Well, why do you take this stuff?" because I was curious. And he said: "Because I blow more notes into my horn when I'm on it. I get anxious before I go to the stage to blow my horn. I take some marijuana. Then I get up there and blow it and I get in more notes in the same amount of time."

I was skeptical, so I said: "Did you ever listen to your music on tape recordings later, when you were sober?" And he said: "Yes." I said: "How was it?" And he said: "It stank."

You see? You get the illusion that it's good. That's your experience. But what does it prove about the universe?

Kanitz: You also mentioned insight this morning. You said that in going back in your life, to a feeling taking you back, that you can usually find a place where you remember a "traumatic" incident, but there probably were a number of unremembered prior incidents.

Ellis: Yes. You experience that: "My mother severely criticized me when I was three, and I was traumatized." You say: "Ah-hah." You're very happy with this "insight." But, you've forgotten the prior events. You fail to recall that most probably she often did so before. How do you know that was the *first* time? You only know it was a *dramatic* time. And without many previous undramatic experiences, would this one you remember really have been "traumatic?"

6. Can the client grow and develop his self or does he become a copy of the therapist?

Ellis: I object to the word "self" here. It isn't that he develops his "self." He developes his *traits.* He posits some basic values that he wants to live by, and he disputes, he minimizes his philosophies that interfere with those values. Then he develops the traits or sub-values he wants. For example, if he wants to be a good musician, he surrenders the views that he can't play well, and studies and practices music.

Practically all therapists are trying to help clients achieve a philosophy consistent with and practical for their basic, chosen values. Some people falsely say: "Ellis is trying to get clients to achieve *his* values, the therapist's values." No, I am trying to help him achieve his, the client's values.

Clients could want to be miserable and I could teach them how to be miserable, because I'm a scientist and have efficient techniques to offer. They practically never do want to be miserable, but they might. Or they might want to be happy homosexuals. And I could show them how to be self-accepting, happy homosexuals, though I'm not homosexual.

So, it is wrong to attribute to rational-emotive therapists a special set of values which they force onto their clients. That's not what we do. We try to get them to achieve their own basic values.

7. Concerning the rightness of the therapist's decisions for the client, are irrational and rational absolute terms? Must rational for the therapist be rational for the client?

Ellis: The answer is: "No." There are no absolutes that we accept. I quoted Shible's *Philosophical Pictures* today. There are, as far as we know, no absolutes.

Rationality means that after I start with certain values, goals, and purposes, I try to efficiently (rationally) achieve them. It's just a technique. It doesn't exist in itself.

About the "rightness of the therapist's decisions for the clients." We don't normally make decisions for clients. That is their prerogative. We ask, "What are your goals, decisions? Now we will help you try to achieve them." If they are indecisive, we help them surrender their irrational ideas — especially, "I must always make a perfect decision!" But, we hope they make decisions for *themselves* and not to please us!

We're not making decisions. We're showing clients their decisions or actions are two kinds, rational and irrational, depending on what *their* goals are, and that they'd better give up the irrational ones. But, they don't *have* to!

8. Does an individual primarily "think" one's way through that part of life which is, frequently, "irrational" (e.g., joy, sadness, loneliness, etc.)?

Ellis: Again, I think Arbuckle means: "Do you give up sadness and joy and fear?" If that's what he means, the answer is "No," because sadness, joy, and fear would usually be beneficial emotions.

You're afraid of something because you may be harmed. You're sad because you don't like the results you're getting and want to change them. You're joyous because you are pleased with what is happening and want to stay pleased.

"Loneliness," I would be a little more skeptical about. It has two parts: 1) rational — "I don't like being alone," and 2) irrational — "What a crumb I am for being alone! How awful!" So, we help people keep the first part and give up the second.

Again, we would distinguish between appropriate and inappropriate emotions, and try to get people to change the inappropriate ones. But there is no absolute here, because people individually differ. Somebody might want to be sadder than somebody else. Others want to be happier. We help them get the emotional responses they truly seem to want.

9. With regard to the RET claim that it has a 90% success ratio, does success mean cure or improvement? What are its criteria for success?

Ellis: First of all, success normally means improvement. I don't think anybody gets totally cured.

Morris: That's what you meant when you talked at today's workshop about getting the client to be less disturbable as a goal in RET.

Ellis: Right. Now ideally we are trying to get clients to be less disturbable for the rest of their lives rather than merely less disturbed today. Ideally!

For example, they are impotent. They want to be potent. They get potent, in a few sessions sometimes. They leave. Now I would try to show them: "Aren't you afraid of failure in other areas besides sex? Would you like to work at being less anxious in those areas, too?"

Kanitz: In other areas of their life?

Ellis: Yes. But they might not want that. So that's their choice.

So success means improvement in the presenting symptom; and, ideally, in general disturbability. But it may just be in symptom. And usually, in studies of therapy, only the symptom is investigated, not disturbability. I don't think anybody has done that kind of study. But decreased disturbability would be our goal.

10. What evidence is available that the client loses his anxiety, depression, fears, etc. and replaces them with effective living, happiness, rational behavior, independence, responsibility and self-actualization?

Ellis: Well, you have lots of different evidences, but none of them absolute. Nobody has solved this problem. In doing studies of psychotherapy, researchers haven't as yet hit upon any definitive, measurable criteria.

We have client self-reports, of course, which are important. They are behaving differently, which can be observed. We have others' observations of them — friends, wives, husbands, children, etc. The important thing would be to discover, when the same obnoxious situation occurs in their lives (for example, somebody excoriates them or they fail at something important), how they newly react.

You see, that would be evidence of their less disturbability.

Not only did they get rid of the anxiety they came with, but they reported: "This week my mate really acted very badly," and they're obviously not depressed or hostile about it.

Morris: In regard to the success ratio, what is the amount of recidivism for your clients?

Ellis: A small percentage of recidivism as against a larger percentage for most other forms of therapy. Arnold Lazarus did a study of his clients when he did Wolpean systematic desensitization and found ninety percent, five years later, fell back. The ten percent who didn't reacquire their symptoms had changed their basic philosophy, which is the premise of RET.

So there seems to be a small percentage of recidivists, closer to maybe fifteen to twenty percent. But we don't exactly know, because we rarely follow-up with detailed interviews. We do send out follow-up questionnaires. "How did you like the therapy? How are you doing now?" Of those coming back, there's only a small percent who revert. They usually require only a few sessions of RET to improve significantly again.

11. If Ellis' arguments about the client's helplessness, dependence and self-discouragement are valid, it would seem that there is less chance for non-directive or less directive methods to work and be successful. Yet, they are. How is this explained by Ellis?

Ellis: Well, they don't work too well. My hypothesis is that, at best, they get people to *feel better*, but not *get better*. So they really don't work that elegantly.

"If less directive methods do work, how is this explained?" Well, first of all, "non-directive" methods are more directive than they claim they are. They are doing many highly active-directive things.

Research showed years ago that Carl Rogers' people are really reinforcing with their "uh-huhs." They are quite directive in their philosophy because they are leading people in certain pathways rather than other pathways, never at random.

And, they have a lot of hidden rationality! If you read de Loreto's study *Comparative Psychotherapy*, where he used RET, Rogerian, and systematic desensitization therapy, the systematic desensitization had a lot of RET in it and the Rogerian method also included a lot of stuff that was close to RET.

My hypothesis is that the clients who really get better with the Rogerian method read a great deal. They read Carl Rogers and other existentially-oriented authors. And, somebody could do a Ph.D. thesis testing the hypothesis that if you read Carl Rogers and also receive non-directive or Rogerian therapy, you come off much better than if you just get therapy, without the reading.

12. RET is extreme in the extent and detail of the values it imposes on its clients.

Ellis: As I said before, it doesn't impose basic values. It helps clients achieve their own values. People may *see* RET as imposing, but that's because they have a non-directive framework and they are prejudiced within the confines of that framework.

13. It appears that RET deals only, or too extensively, with thinking, cognition and rational behavior. It seems to neglect the emotions.

Ellis: Well, that's nonsense because we invariably begin with C, the *emotional* consequence. And we use many techniques, such as rational-emotive imagery, that are largely to help people get in touch with, acknowledge, and change their emotions. We give them many kinds of encounter, shame-attacking, risk-taking, role playing, non-verbal, and other emotive-evocative-dramatic exercises.

RET is more concrete and specific about thinking than most other therapies are, but it doesn't neglect emotions. The goal is to change depression, anxiety, self-hatred and hatred of others. And, of course, it discriminates between appropriate and inappropriate emotions more than other systems do. So it deals very much with the emotions. It may not over-emphasize methods dealing with the emotions, but that is because it deliberately uses many cognitive and behavioristic, as well as emotive, techniques.

14. The importance of the client-therapist relationship appears to be neglected or unimportant.

Ellis: That's not true, either. First of all, in psychoanalytic terms, if we find "transference," we analyze and uproot it. If clients think they *need* the love of the therapist, which is what "transference" is mainly about, we show them that they don't need that love, and that if they deify their therapist, that is part of their disturbance.

We use a great deal of relationship-modeling, because RET therapists rarely feel upset and hurt when clients act badly to them, do not get angry, and do not usually get neurotically involved in the therapeutic process. Instead, they consciously try to use themselves as good models in the client-therapist relationship.

Unconditional self-acceptance of clients is shown in the course of RET sessions. The therapist shows clients, no matter what they do, they're not lice or jerks. Where other therapists may do this too, in RET we also actively teach clients to fully accept themselves. So, we add some important aspects to the client-therapist relationship.

We are not usually terribly supportive, in the usual sense, of patting clients on the back, telling them they're great people, or that we like them. We don't emphasize that aspect of the client-therapist relationship. We would think that warmth may actually be harmful rather than helpful, because it may lead clients up the garden path. We do use various supportive aspects of the client-therapist relationship and, of course, we think we do so more efficiently than many other therapies do.

15. It appears that Ellis is not aware of, or concerned about the possibility that direct attacks on and confrontations directed at resistance can be viewed by the client as a threat. This would then lead to an increase in the resistance and make change either more difficult or impossible.

Ellis: Well, the problem is whether clients really do often increase their resistance. Rational-emotive therapists are not attacking *them,* but attacking their *ideas* about themselves, which is the cause of their resistance.

And, if we're successful, as we fairly quickly often are, in getting them not to damn themselves for anything, then their resistance tends to minimize or vanish. And, they rarely construe our attack on their self-defeating philosophies as an attack on them. If they did, we'd show them the error of that interpretation and teach them the elements of self-forgiveness.

Morris: Glasser is fairly well known for illustrating some of his methods for coping with the client's resistance by saying: "You appear right now not to be ready or willing. Leave now and come back when you are ready." Would you, for example, use that type of technique or response?

Ellis: Only in extreme cases. We try various evocative methods first. For example, we had a woman, just the other day, in one of my groups. She was new in the group, so I said to her, after several other people spoke, "Will you please tell us something about your problems?" She said: "Oh, I'm not ready to do that. I just came to listen the first few times." Before I could do anything, a couple of other members jumped in and said: "Why aren't you ready? What are you afraid of? What do you think will happen if you tell us some gory things about yourself?" Within, I'd say, five minutes at most, she was embroiled in talking about her problems.

If she really persisted, the group might push her too hard and I might stop them. If she seemed to have strong resistance, I might say: "Well, sit there for several sessions and we won't bother you. When you want to talk up, do so."

But, most of the time, we would persuade resistant clients by showing them that nothing terrible would happen if they opened up. You see, Glasser omits the point of eliminating the irrational *ideas* behind resistances. If clients say: "Well, I don't want to tell you certain things," I'd say: "What do you think would actually happen if you did tell me those things?"

People come up to the stage to demonstrate at our regular Friday night public workshops and they often say: "I'm anxious right now." So we talk about it, what they're telling themselves right then and there to *make* themselves anxious. Then they become unanxious. Then they go on to speak about other intimate problems. So, we don't do what Dr. Glasser does with resistance.

"What's resistance?" We say to clients: "You *tell yourself something* to make yourself resistant. What do you think will occur if you open up? That the world will come to an end? That your audience will only think of you, and despise you, for the next fifty years? Is that *likely?* And if people do criticize you, *must* you agree with them and view yourself as a louse?"

Kanitz: The client might walk away and think of other things that might be terrible if you don't deal with them right there.

Ellis: Right. You're quite right. He may be traumatized. If you let him get away with resisting, he may leave the session and say: "What a jerk I am! I didn't speak up to the group or to Ellis. I wasted my time!" I've had people do that.

16. Is RET effective for the reason Ellis believes?

Ellis: That's an almost impossible question to answer because, if it's effective, and we have lots of studies now showing it is, you can't easily say *why* it is.

I have all kinds of hypotheses, for example, why the non-cognitive therapies sometimes work. I contend they unwittingly help clients change their cognitions.

Critics can say the same thing about RET: That we think we're changing clients' cognitions, but really they (the clients) think the RET therapist loves them and *that's* why they change.

You would have a hard time definitively answering Patterson's question. You would probably have to do all kinds of studies, which would better be done.

17. In what ways is it effective? Does it achieve the same kinds of results as other systems?

Ellis: Yes and no. For one thing, as I said before, we think that clients *get* better in RET rather than merely *feel* better: that they become less disturbable and conditionable. You see, we are one of the few therapies that use clients' conditionability to help change their cognitions. As you saw in my demonstration of rational-emotional imagery today, we can use operant conditioning quite often.

But we're also trying to teach clients to be less conditionable, in the sense of giving less of a damn what other people think of them. If we *just* reinforce them all the time, especially by social approval, that could be deadly. They'd change their behaviors — stop smoking, for example — but still think they *need* other people's love. How nutty!

"In what ways is RET effective?" In some same and in some different ways from other therapies. Virtually all therapists try to help change clients' behavior; all, I think, try to show them that they are not dirt.

But we try to do so more concretely, directly, and elegantly; and to encourage clients to be less conditionable and less disturbable in the future. That's our goal. We may not achieve it, but it is our goal.

18. Does RET end in client independence and responsibility?

Ellis: As far as we can tell, it definitely does. First of all, we were one of the pioneers of assertion training. Not only women, but men. We especially encourage women, as our administrative director, Janet L. Wolfe, and as Patricia Jakubowski-Spector have noted in papers and in workshops, to ask for things (including sex!) they never asked for before; to take the initiative in socializing; to resist the emotional blackmail of their parents and mates, etc. RET helps them to take more responsibility for their own behavior.

Of course, we show most clients how to stop copping out and to stop saying: "My mother made me" or "the situation made me." So RET notably leads to independence and responsibility.

If somebody had a good test of independence, which I don't recall there really is, I think our clients would come out very high on it. Reality therapy clients would probably do pretty well on responsibility, too. We are always teaching self-discipline.

Morris: In terms of responsibility, is one of the learnings of most RET clients self-responsibility?

Ellis: Yes, two kinds of responsibility.

Morris: The idea, "I'm responsible for my own self? I'm responsible for my own actions and my own reactions?"

Ellis: Right. We teach that "I'm responsible for my own actions."

But then the other kind of responsibility is "You will probably get future rewards mainly by taking responsibility for your own discipline today." We teach *long-range* hedonism. Also: "Since you decided to live in a social group — you don't *have* to, but you obviously decided to do so — you'd *better* be responsible to the group and not do unto others what you wouldn't want them to do unto you." So we teach social responsibility or what Adler called social interest.

19. Does client change or improvement persist?

Ellis: First of all, I quote Arnold Lazarus' study where he studied systematic desensitization clients, and found that about ninety percent fell back after five years to their old phobia or other disordered behaviors; while the ten percent that changed their philosophic outlook didn't fall back. We find the same thing. Once you really change your basic irrational cognitions, you may fall back, I'm not saying you can't, but you have much less of a chance to do so.

We have several studies that show that when RET and another kind of therapy, like desensitization or Rogerian therapy, are effective, the RET clients fall back less.

General Questions About RET

The following are general questions about RET and its techniques which were responded to by Albert Ellis during a RET

Workshop held in Macomb, Illinois, (Ellis, 1974b). It must be emphasized that responses four through fourteen are *paraphrases* from the authors' tapes and are *not* direct quotes from Ellis.

1. How does the element of interview structure by the therapist affect the client-therapist relationship?

Ellis: Well, because of the structure implicit in RET, the relationship tends to be less personal to some degree. Not completely, but some RET time is didactic and, therefore, not overly personal. Less "transference" exists in RET: transference from the past to the present, or the deifying of the therapist so that clients easily fall in love with him or her.

I am not ultra-sympathetic to my clients, but they often say, "I feel very understood." They also report, "I have read *A Guide to Rational Living* and never understood myself so well." This in spite of the fact that *A Guide to Rational Living* hardly provides real empathy.

The RET therapist may use planned support, because he is planning, plotting, and scheming in his head to help the client in all feasible ways. So there may be more planned support than there is in some forms of therapy. If clients are severely depressed or suicidal we can, with our structure, deliberately show them good things about themselves; we can demonstrate what they can do; and we can be otherwise highly supportive. But we don't overemphasize warmth because it can easily encourage a dire need for love. Anyway, there are several ways in which RET affects the client-therapist relationship, (Ellis, 1974a).

2. How necessary or important in RET theory are dynamics such as empathy, trust, positive regard and acceptance?

Ellis: Positive regard, or what I call acceptance of self-acceptance, is very important, meaning philosophically. It's not that I have to like you; but I accept, and refrain from damning, all humans and all clients. And I show that in my behavior and teaching. Empathy, in RET, can be understanding, not just feeling with a client. Clients actually do tend to trust us because we are authoritative. Not authoritarian, but authoritative. So they trust us to be on their side, to be helpful. But not trust in the sense that many encounter groups use the term: "I need to trust you and I'm not going to tell you anything before I trust you." Actually, I do engender a lot of trust. Because if I use my usual four-letter-word vocabulary and freely am myself, clients do trust me and bring out things they wouldn't as quickly tell other, stiffer-necked therapists.

Kanitz: So you would have an acceptance of the person, but probably would reject, or definitely would reject inappropriate belief systems that he or she presents?

Ellis: Right! We would reject their *belief systems*, but fully accept *them*. Now the question is: is that real acceptance? The Rogerians would say, "Oh no, clients are going to resist if you attack their beliefs." Even the Freudians would agree: "They are going to resist." We say you *can* attack clients' ideas. Because we are not arguing with *them*, but with their *belief systems*.

Morris: In regard to that question, are there any necessary or sufficient conditions for RET? Rogers lists his six for example.

Ellis: No, he lists them for all psychotherapy. I wrote an article against his original paper. I think some of it is in *Reason and Emotion in Psychotherapy*. I show that there are *no* necessary and sufficient conditions for therapy because a person can radically change his philosophy and behavior by doing transcendental meditation (which is really a diversionary technique); or by believing in Christian Science; or by reading a book; or by many other unorthodox forms of "therapy." You see, I think the main element of psychotherapy is philosophic reconstruction. And we don't know exactly why people philosophically reconstruct. They often do it without knowing *how* they do it, and they get better. So I don't see any *necessary* and *sufficient* conditions for psychotherapy.

Morris: Granted, for psychotherapy as a profession. What about RET?

Ellis: Well, we would not call it Rational-Emotive Therapy unless it had 1) a significant element of cognitive persuasion, teaching, and information-giving; and 2) a sizable element of cognitive-behavioral homework assignments. RET involves presenting the cognitive-behavioral methods of personality change, often in a dramatic form.

We have one vector in RET which is called strength of belief. People strongly hold onto their beliefs. An RET therapist, therefore, vigorously intervenes and tries to get people to strongly, powerfully contradict their irrational, self-defeating ideas. If these things are not done, it's hardly RET, though it may be psychotherapy. Rogers held that there are necessary and sufficient conditions, such as relationship, for *all* effective psychotherapy, not merely for Rogerian therapy or RET. And I still feel, twenty years later, that he was distinctly wrong (Ellis, 1974a).

3. Will you comment on the theory that letting anger out is cathartic and, eventually, leads to a lessening in hostility?

Ellis: We have lots of evidence that it does more harm than good to let anger out instead of getting at its causes and minimizing hostility. Daniel Casriel is one of the main therapists in New York who teaches clients to scream, whine, and vent their anger. I had a client I was seeing individually, whom Dan was seeing in group. The client was getting less anxious as I talked with him; but he told me, "Every time I attend a Casriel group, I get more hostile." He finally quit this group and became unanxious and unangry. Many therapists teach their clients to express hostility on the theory that eventually they will become less hostile. But I think the evidence is that they usually become more so (Ellis, 1974a).

4. If you minimize the client's disturbability, aren't you eliminating feeling?

Ellis: No. You try to get rid of *inappropriate* feelings. You get the client, once he changes his irrational beliefs, to feel regret, sorrow, annoyance, and so forth. These are definite, even negative, *feelings*. However, he will tend to have appropriate feeling, not *inappropriate* ones. For example, he trades anger and rage for irritation. But he still *feels*.

5. What maintains the "nutty" ideas? Why don't we change?

Ellis: First, because they are not completely ungratifying. They do have immediate reward. For example, short range hedonism and immediate gain versus future pain, (smoking, procrastination about one's term paper, boozing, etc.). You tend, once you start a behavior, to carry it on. This is similar to Allport's concept of functional autonomy.

6. Is it usual for the client to resist in revealing his "B" sentences?

Ellis: Not as usual as it is for clients who volunteer for public demonstrations. Other clients resist because they are sometimes looking for something abstruse. The actual B sentence is often so obvious and simple that they sometimes can't believe they have found it. Almost anyone can find his step B sentences, especially if he is trained to do so. Very frequently, my clients worry: "Will I get it?" However, that usually goes away after a short period of time, and they learn to zero in quickly on their irrational beliefs.

7. Does change in behavior lead to different cognition?

Ellis: Yes, frequently. For example, you can be afraid of water. You can force yourself to jump in and eventually you can lose your cognition that "I'll drown." You can also be forced to jump in. If your mother threw you in the water enough times, you would probably change your cognition. Action often leads to cognitive restructuring and change.

8. How do you approach individual variability, which is mainly biological, of the person's reaction to situations and feelings?

Ellis: We don't usually try. We don't argue with the degree of reaction to a stimulus. We are concerned with the *magical* part of the reaction; those times when you say "I must" or "I should." We do not argue with your value system, what you like or dislike. We argue with statements like "I *can't stand* what I don't like." That is the magic we attack.

9. Aren't you implying that all the client has to do is assume he's good and not justify his goodness by his behavior?

Ellis: I used to, in the original edition of *A Guide to Rational Living,* I later realized however, that saying "I'm alive and, therefore, I am good" can work pragmatically, but not philosophically. Somebody else can say "Prove you're good because you're alive. I think you're rotten because you're alive." You can't prove either one. You can't prove you are good. You can't prove you are bad.

I realized you do not have to prove either statement. You don't have to rate yourself. You had better rate your deeds and acts in accordance with how well they meet the basic goals you chose. You can't accurately rate a process, which is what the "self" is, for it has a past, a present, and a (largely unpredictable) future. As L. S. Barnsdale has noted, "You are not your actions. You are that which acts." And how can you really rate or give a report card to *that which acts?*

10. Is failure necessary?

Ellis: Glasser says no. Children fail and feel terrible and worthless. Therefore, let's have schools without failure. That is inane. The children will grow up and meet failure in society and fall on their faces. Life is a series of failures. I don't see how to eliminate *all* failure.

At the Living School we teach the children to fail and to learn to cope rationally with it. We give them failure exercises as homework and they learn it is not *awful* to fail, it is merely inconvenient.

11. What are the differences between RET and Gestalt?

Ellis: First, the similarities. Both, along with Karen Horney, believe in the tyranny of the "shoulds." Both get the client to replace the word "can't" with "won't." Both keep people in the here and now, believing the past is a cop-out.

Now, the differences. First, they concentrate heavily on dreams. We do not. We stick with real behavior.

Second, they believe that if you are fully aware of what you do, you will change. We have evidence that that is not true.

Third, they are more interested in developing client awareness than in client change.

Fourth, they never clearly defined the difference between appropriate and inappropriate emoting. They teach you to be more hostile because they wrongly confuse a hostile feeling with an assertive feeling. Assertion is great. Anger is not. Anger includes a "shalt" or a "should." Experiments show that expressing anger leads to more anger. If catharting anger worked, it should also work for anxiety, frustration, and so on; we believe it does not work.

12. How is RET similar to Adlerian therapy?

Ellis: Adler, as we do, believed that man lives by purposes, values, goals, and ideas. He also believed, as RET does, that you can directly question, challenge and attack irrational ideas, not the person who holds them. He was one of the first directive therapists and set some good precedents for RET.

13. When you do something silly in front of people, your rational side frequently says "What do you care? You're not going to see these people again." That makes sense in New York or Chicago, but how about Macomb and other small towns where you will see them again?

Ellis: First, you convince yourself that it is not *awful* that they saw you do something stupid and silly.

Second, you try to avoid doing things that are really penalizing. You recognize what actual penalty or consequence is involved when you do or say things that people disapprove.

Third, you discover that most people will forget or not remember for very long what you did, in spite of your belief that they will.

The most important element is to *selectively* pick what you are going to do. That is why we tell our clients not to do things that will get them arrested, cause them to lose their job, get thrown out of school, and so on, in the course of their shame attacking exercises.

14. Will you comment on premature attenuation of the negative feeling?

Ellis: That is a danger in RET. The Freudians believe that no pain equals no motivation. They are partly right. We quickly alleviate the initial pain and the client may quit coming. So the problem is to get him or her to continue therapy in spite of pain attenuation, until a more elegant and continuing solution is attained.

15. Will you comment on blaming yourself for blaming?

Ellis: That's what we combat. Because you not only condemn yourself for failing, but you then realize that you are wrong about self-condemning. So you often condemn yourself for condemning yourself. Or condemn yourself for condemning yourself for condemning yourself!

Kanitz: The skillful therapist can pick that up!

Ellis: Yes, we have it in our theory. We suspect right away that if people have free floating or pandemic anxiety, they are really anxious about *being* anxious. That is one of their main problems. Consequently, I get them to look at their anxiety about *being* anxious; to find and to dispute their awfulizing beliefs; and to surrender these irrational ideas. Later, we go back to the original anxiety, and to the philosophies behind it, and to disputing and eliminating *those* self-defeating beliefs.

RET tackles anxiety — or self damning — on three major levels: 1) "I may fail at something — and wouldn't that be awful!" 2) I may fail at being unanxious — and wouldn't *that* be terrible!" 3) "I may fail at psychotherapy — and wouldn't *that* be horrible." RET helps clients discover that *nothing* is truly awful, terrible, or horrible — but only highly uncomfortable, obnoxious, or inconvenient.

Summary and Synopsis

It is apparent that Ellis and RET have had a significant impact on psychotherapy. The amount of response generated by Ellis and his writings is evidence that therapists and other professionals realize RET is a serious system and cannot be ignored. It has not, and will not, disappear if one pretends it is not there.

The great majority of responses concerning RET are neutral, negative, and doubting. Most concentrate on the belief that the RET therapist imposes values, ignores the affective domain, or ignores the effect of the client's background and environment. These and other questions were responded to by Ellis, with the result being that 1) imposition of values is not done; 2) the affect (or feeling) is the starting point; and 3) the environment is accepted as a contributing factor but only mildly emphasized, because humans cognitively create their own scripts. They are not created *for* them by others or by the environment.

On the positive side, it is difficult to argue with RET's success rate and low percentage of recidivism. The RET emphasis on cognition and its control of individual emotions appear, to us, to be among its major contributions. We hope that other practitioners would adopt the RET therapy goal, that clients would preferably *get* better, not merely *feel* better.

Regardless of whether one agrees or disagrees with RET, it offers a wide variety of techniques which can be utilized. Its concept of graduated homework is an important contribution. Any therapist could utilize the homework technique. It helps overcome a great deterrent to therapeutic success, the client's unwillingness or failure to do anything outside of the session. It also helps the therapist determine whether the client is improving behaviorally. For these reasons, we urge the reader to consider its utilization and not reject it because it is too directive and/or violates one's therapy values and beliefs.

Ellis' willingness to grant the authors an interview is an indication of his sincerity and *belief* that he and his theory *are* correct and can stand the test. He *lives* his theory. He *is* RET. He may not be totally correct. He is certainly not totally erroneous. He is, instead, open, honest, and sincere. If such traits result from belief in RET, we had better all look at it, evaluate it, and incorporate into our being all that is compatible with it.

4

Research Results and
Related Literature

Evidence supporting the effectiveness of RET as a treatment method is quite abundant. Ellis and his associates are currently compiling a research bibliography of over 300 studies. The authors strongly urge the reader, be he or she supportive or critical of RET, to obtain this forthcoming research volume (Ellis and Budd, 1975). We will, however, review some of the evidence found in various publications.

Research Results

There appear to be two main questions which critics of RET ask: (1) where is the proof that human thinking and cognition is the cause of feeling and emotion, and that changing cognition leads to change in emotional reaction; and (2) where is the evidence that RET, as a treatment approach, is effective?

When Ellis (1956) first delineated the theory and principles of RET there was little, if any, evidence that his hypotheses and assumptions were correct. Since that time, there have appeared many studies and a vast amount of literature supporting the RET emphasis upon cognition as the cause of disturbance and dysfunction.

Proof that man thinks himself into his emotional reactions and can think himself out of them appears in Beck (1959, 1967, 1970); Becker (1960); Becker, et al. (1963); Carlson, et al. (1969); Davies (1970); Davison (1965, 1967, 1969); Deane (1966); Frank (1968); Glass, et al. (1969); Jones (1968); Lang, et al. (1967); Nisbett and Schacter (1966); Schacter and Singer (1962); Taft (1965); Valins (1966); Valins and Ray (1967); and Zingle (1965).

Dua (1970) studied the use of behaviorally-oriented action and psychotherapy re-education on variables such as introversion and extroversion. His finding was that the action-oriented program, which used behavioral contracts, operant conditioning, etc., was more effective in reducing attitudinal changes than was the re-education program.

Ellis (1957b) investigated the use of RET, orthodox analysis, and psychoanalytically-oriented psychotherapy. His study showed that the results of the application of RET were significantly different from the results of the other two systems. Glicken (1968) studied the use of RET as a system of short-term therapy. He isolated the clients' irrational ideas, then challenged them, and finally helped the clients to learn to cope with their illogicalness. He found such an approach to be successful in eighty to ninety percent of the cases typically confronted by mental health workers.

Trexler (1972) studied the use of RET, placebo, and no-treatment on public speaking anxiety. His results heavily support the effectiveness of RET over the placebo and no-treatment approaches in eliminating public speaking anxieties.

Rimm and Litvak (1969) measured subjects' emotional responses to affectively "loaded" sentences and affectively neutral sentences. They attempted to support Ellis' theory relating implicit verbalization to emotional arousal. The result indicating that two out of three subjects showed significantly greater emotional responses to the "loaded" sentences was viewed as partially supportive of the Ellis theory.

Karst and Trexler (1970) attempted to reduce public speaking anxiety. They used three treatment groups, giving the first fixed roles, the second rational-emotive group therapy, and the third no treatment. Both groups receiving therapy improved. However, there was no significant difference between the RET method and the fixed role group. Karst concluded that cognitive therapies, such as RET, are amenable to controlled study if clear definition of variables is obtained.

Rand (1970) discovered that RET group therapy was effective as an approach to overcoming academic underachievement. Other studies support RET as a treatment system of high efficiency and effectiveness. Among these are Ard (1967, 1968, 1969); Breen (1970); Callahan (1967); Diamond (1967); di Loreto (1969); Glicken (1966); Grossack (1965); Gullo (1966); Hauck (1966, 1967, 1968); and Sherman (1967).

There is another series of research results which indicate that certain RET techniques are efficient and successful. The importance of these studies lies in the fact that they investigate techniques such as graduated homework, rational-emotive imagery, bibliotherapy, etc. If the technique works, one could use it regardless of one's philosophical orientation.

Graduated homework has been studied by Ellis (1967c) and Maultsby (1971b). Both report significant effects with *in vivo* desensitization, indicating that homework assignments facilitate and expedite client improvement. Fox (1971) and Carios (1972) designed tests and inventories based on RET principles. Both discovered that such instruments aid the client in discovering his irrational sentences and facilitate the improvement process. Maultsby (1970) indicates that the routine use of tape recording during RET sessions positively affects the therapy.

Garfield (1967) and Litvak (1969) studied snake anxiety and snake avoidance behavior. Garfield used desensitization based on reciprocal inhibition with one group and *in vivo* training with the phobic object with another group. The group members receiving *in vivo* training achieved a greater relative change in their phobic behavior than the other group. Litvak's results supported Garfield's. He used systematic desensitization versus *in vivo* desensitization and discovered that contact desensitization was significantly superior.

Other supportive studies concerning RET techniques include Cooke (1966); Maultsby (1968); Ritter (1968); and Zajonc (1968).

Related Literature

There is a large amount of literature which supports RET as a therapy system. It is not feasible to report on all of these, but some do warrant special consideration.

Maultsby (1971a) discusses rational-emotive imagery (REI) and recommends that it be used as a self-help exercise by the client between sessions. REI requires that the client recreate, in his mind, an incident which usually results in irrational behavior. He is to spend ten to thirty minutes per day fantasizing this incident and cognitively changing his reaction so that it is more rational and logical. REI will often, according to Maultsby, aid the client in learning new, more rational and desirable, responses to a given situation.

Meichenbaum (1973) suggests the use of behavior therapy techniques to help clients modify what they say to themselves (the step B internalized sentences). He feels that a variety of techniques can be effective. Among these are modeling, conditioning imagery, cognitive rehearsal, and operant conditioning.

Ellis and Blum (1967) delineate rational training as a method for facilitating management and labor relations. They stress the fact that rational training differs from the traditional methods employed in management training courses. It employs directiveness, a high degree of structure, and homework assignments. The purposes of rational training are to show the group members how to eliminate fear of failure, how to be more tolerant, how to gain their own self-acceptance, and how to achieve a higher tolerance of frustration.

Laughridge (1972) discusses handling resistance to interpretation. His belief is that the client who tends to rate his/her self is extremely resistant to the therapist's interpretation of his irrational thinking and behavior. Such a client has a tendency to distort the interpretation and turn it into an added self-damning sentence, such as: "Look at the derogatory things he said about me. I must be terrible." Laughridge employed, quite successfully, the following technique: (1) he pointed to an empty chair and told the client: "Sit quietly while I tell Dr. So and So why our previous session's conversation was so fruitless."; (2) he then told the fantasy therapist about the client's unwillingness to listen and hear his verbalizations, playing sections of the previous week's tape to support his hypotheses; (3) at the end of the session, Laughridge discovered that the client, by being forced to passively *listen,* learned how he/she *had* distorted his previous statements.

Kempel (1973) delineates means of identifying the client who will prematurely self-terminate therapy. He suggests that the therapist openly discuss with the client the premature termination issue. During this discussion, the therapist should help the client recognize how he *might* irrationally talk himself out of returning. Kempel cautions that the confrontation with the client is *only* used to investigate possible irrational sentences used to support early termination. It is not to be used to coerce, evaluate, blame, or make the client feel guilty.

Knaus (1973) discusses the application of rational-emotive theory and technique to overcoming procrastination. He shows that the procrastinator delays in two major areas, self-development and self-maintenance. He usually does this by holding one (or both) of two illogical, irrational views: (1) that he is inadequate; and (2) that the world is too hard, demanding, and difficult. He also discusses the use of rationalization, impulsivity, and escapism by the individual to resist change. Among the techniques used to overcome procrastination are: (1) *begin now* — you need not wait for inspiration from the Holy Ghost or that magical moment of inspiration; (2) *look for your internal sentences* — you are saying something silly, irrational, and illogical so find it and dispute it; (3) *self-reinforcement* — use operant conditioning, and punish yourself for continuing to delay and reward yourself for accomplishing; (4) *written reminders* — make up cards with sayings on them such as "Don't let the grass grow under you," or "Today is *the* day," and read them each day.

Trexler (1973) discusses his RET approach to dealing with suicidal clients. He says you must first make sure how serious the client's depression and suicidal tendencies are. Then, track down with the client his irrational beliefs and help depropagandize them. Trexler says that most suicidal clients "catastrophize, demand perfection of themselves and others, believe that external events and past experiences cause their misery, and are often emotionally dependent on others." Frequently, other hatred is an important component and should be confronted. Trexler finally discusses "postmortem guilt." What do you, the therapist, do when you lose a client? Trexler urges the adoption of a rational belief system. Your words, interactions, interpretations, etc., can, at worst, be only partly responsible for the client's suicide. At worst! However, you are *never* guilty for it! The client is always responsible for what he does with *his* life, not you.

Concluding Comments

This chapter has briefly indicated those articles and studies which: (1) support the RET hypothesis that cognition and thinking are the core of human disturbance and dysfunction; (2) indicate that RET is a reliable, effective, and efficient therapeutic system; (3) discuss and/or study RET techniques concerning their application and efficiency; (4) relate to RET and discuss or delineate relevant principles and issues.

We have purposefully attempted to reduce our previously heavy concentration on the writings of Albert Ellis. Instead, we wished to expose the reader to the studies and writings of other professionals.

Ellis' contributions are enormous and should be considered by the reader. We refer the reader to the selected readings and resources at the end of this monograph and strongly encourage perusal of Ellis' writings.

It is our belief that sufficient evidence exists to support RET as a reputable, effective system of counseling and therapy. We realize that most of the readers will say: "Yes, I agree. It is fine if that's where you are coming from. I, myself, choose *not* to pursue RET." We do not want the reader to abandon his therapeutic orientation. We do, however, hope (and encourage) that the professionals reading this monograph will be open to the use of some of the RET techniques. There is abundant evidence that graduated homework, rational-emotive imagery, bibliotherapy, and other RET techniques are useful. One can use RET techniques without being an Ellisian. We paraphrase the TV slogan: "Try them, you'll like them."

5

Issues, Activities, and Applications — Current and Future

The focus of this chapter is upon the issues, activities, and applications of RET, especially in regard to emotions, the Living School, and rational encounter groups. We cite the possibility of future applications and discuss the general educational goals of rational-emotive theory. The notion that the principles of RET have a great deal to offer children and adults in their emotional development is an important facet in this chapter. The plight of the aged is also given thoughtful consideration in terms of the suggested application of RET basics.

Issues, Activities, and Applications — Current

The issues of today, in terms of RET, have persisted for the past twenty years or more. Which emotions are appropriate or inappropriate to effective human living, the nature of man, emotive therapeutic approaches, operant conditioning, building the therapist-client relationship, and the development of the educational model all remain issues. In an interview with Dr. Ellis (1974a), an elaboration of the current issues in RET was provided to the authors. The following is an excerpt from that interview.

What are the current issues in RET?

Ellis: One is the issue I spoke about today, covering appropriate emotions, both negative and positive. We take certain positive emotions, like elation or grandiosity, and we say they are sometimes inappropriate. Joy can be inappropriate if you're killing people and getting joy out of it, because it's against other basic human values. But we especially take the negative emotions and divide them clearly into appropriate and inappropriate feelings. So, that's an issue.

The value of a human being, which came up today, is another important problem. We teach that there is *no* intrinsic value. At least, I do. You're not good because you're alive. You're not bad. You just are. And that's still a rare position, one of teaching clients not to rate themselves, their essences, at all, for therapists to take.

We use today, more than ever, all kinds of emotive approaches, especially in encounter-group RET. So that's an issue: how to use those approaches for rational ends. We do more behavior modification than we used to do, especially operant conditioning, although we always did behavior training, role-playing, modeling, and behavior rehearsal. We have pioneered in *in vivo* homework assignments. We might now use more relaxation methods. We do imagery more than we used to. We used to be mainly cognitive-verbal, now we do cognitive-imagery a good deal more as in rational-emotive imagery (REI).

We do operant conditioning of cognitions. This was pioneered, after I originally suggested it, by Don Meichenbaum of the University of Waterloo. He takes things that people say to themselves, and then he desensitizes them with operant conditioning methods. We have a new technique, cognitive deconditioning that I frequently use with my individual and group clients.

Some RET people spend more time relating warmly to their clients than I often do. They may "hook" them with relating. Since, these therapists think, therapy is going to be a difficult business, why not get clients to relate closely to the therapist? Not because therapists or clients have a dire need for love — we would obviously work against that — but because relating will work temporarily. So we study that aspect of therapy.

A current issue is developing our educational model. With teachers, school children, and adults we are trying to create techniques of RET for wide-scale usage. Ultimately, by using cassettes, films, TV presentations, we hope to take rational-emotive training to the whole public. So those are some of the live issues right now.

It is obvious that these current issues, as presented in the interview, encompass the broad goals of RET. While RET has had what one might call a thorough exposure of its techniques, it remains a radical approach. Naturally, because of its differences from other major psychotherapeutic methods, the theory must stand the test of time. The authors propose the possibility that the pendulum may just now be swinging toward the more directive approaches to counseling and therapy. In the age of accountability, the society in which we live is striving for the realistic assessment of everything and everybody. The philosophy of RET will probably stand strong in its quest to avoid the attempts to turn people into nonhuman or superhuman beings.

The Living School

A pioneering effort is presently underway at the Institute for Advanced Study in Rational Psychotherapy. Innovators have conceived of and operationalized an ungraded school for normal children. The goal of the Living School is to assist children in gaining an understanding of their personal attitudes and feelings. The emphasis is on encouraging emotional well-being in the lives of children, the teachers, and the parents. The idea is to engender emotional education in the school and the home. Emotional education might best be described as the inclusion of the basic principles of sane living, as taught by RET, into the everyday curriculum. By including rational-emotive approaches along with the regular academic requirements, children, teachers, and parents become involved in their own learning process.

The Living School attempts to eliminate intense competition while assisting children with any learning problems that might occur. Learning skills and communication arts, such as reading, writing, mathematics, language arts, and science are required. While personal expression and social interaction are paramount throughout the educational experience, probably the most expressive outlet is through the childrens' involvement in art, drama, literature, and play. The teachers continually assist children in understanding that they create their own upsetting behavior and suggest how they might overcome the consequent anxiety or hostility.

Thus, a premium is placed upon the child becoming aware that learning almost always involves relationships with others and the presence of *intrapersonal* communication. The children are also given failure exercises, designed to help them learn to cope with failure.

The problem-solving abilities of each child are recognized and considered vitally important as each identifies self-actualizing and self-defeating behaviors in self and others. Ellis (1974b) makes the point that the Living School is not for disturbed children, but rather an experimental school where methods are being designed for use in regular community schools.

The school, now in its fifth year, has much to offer those educators interested in RET principles for schools. The following accomplishments are presented as outcomes of the original pioneering efforts in administering the Living School, and are presented to further inform the reader of the experiment. The Living School has accomplished the following:

1. Created learning materials, textbooks, and programmed instruction relevant to emotional education.
2. Created a preparation program for teachers, counselors, administrators, and parents relevant to emotional education.
3. Designed, tested, and refined specific emotional education programs which are applicable to regular community schools.
4. Found more effective methods for handling classroom groups.

This unique experimentation appears to have tremendous implications for rational living, including learning skills in contributing to group decision-making. The school develops a climate which allows individuals to mature and communicate effectively their unique contributions toward change and improvement of self and others. The authors contend that the Living School is a monumental experiment which attempts to incorporate emotional education into the home, the school, and the community. We look forward to the research findings from such a creative endeavor.

Group Work

Encounter groups are considered to be efficient delivery systems for employing a variety of therapeutic techniques. The Institute for Advanced Study in Rational Psychotherapy in New York City has devised a procedure which is called *A Weekend of Rational En-*

counter. After experimenting for two years, this highly structured experience allows each participant to involve himself actively in verbal and non-verbal risk-taking experiences. Problem-solving is centered around supervised attempts by group members to help one another. Encountering irrational beliefs in self and others becomes a therapeutic experience for the individual members. This intensive experience is supportive while allowing members to handle deeper problems and gain feedback from others, usually pertaining to self-defeating beliefs. Since this rational encounter group is a marathon, homework is suggested for each member and is reported back to the group after an eight hour relaxation period between sessions. Any technique may be introduced, depending upon the sophistication of the leader. The following excerpt describes a marathon group under the leadership of Dr. Albert Ellis.

. . . .

For example, one of the women in a recent rational encounter group was shown, on several occasions, that she was only reacting as a therapist in the group, as she did her own work with her patients, and that she was not revealing anything about her personal life because such revelations appeared to be too threatening to her. One of the males in the group chose her to work with and got in the center of the group with her in an attempt to show her how evasive she had been so far during the marathon. With some help from the rest of the group, he finally seemed to be reaching her, and she did admit that she had serious problems of her own but that she felt much more comfortable talking about other people's hangups than she did talking about her own. The group was highly elated, because this therapist member became quite upset, in the course of having her defenses assailed by the others, and began to cry and to admit that she really was, in spite of her seeming composure, a very lonely person, who mainly wanted to achieve a sustained love relationship with a man, and that she had miserably failed to do this as yet. They were all set to sympathize with her, to show her how therapeutic it was for her to admit her real problem, and to let her off the hook.

The leader insisted, however, that she right there and then look for the basic causes of her loneliness and her defensiveness. She said that she had been in psychoanalytic therapy for five years and that she knew these causes: namely, her rejection by her father, when she was a girl, and her insistence since that time that she find a man just like her father to love her and marry her. Her ex-husband and all her main lovers had been, on the contrary, weak men who

were dependent on her, and who were not at all ┃'
and rejecting father.

"Bull!" the leader interjected. "Even if th⌐
life are true, they hardly explain why, first, yo⌐
lutely needed your father's love originally, nor ⌐
are utterly convinced that you still need some 'stro.
proval. What's the *philosophy* or *value system* that you ⌐.
bility had as a child, and are still holding on to, that *ma.*
desperately in need of a rejecting man's love?"

This therapist could only come up with the idea that because h⌐
father had disapproved of her she now needed the acceptance of a
man like him; but the leader insisted that this idea did not explain
her original demand for her father's love. Finally, one of the group
members said: "Don't you really mean that even when you were a
child you strongly believed that if *any* significant figure in your life,
such as your father, disapproved of *you;* and that the only way that
you yourself could possibly accept your being, and think that you
had a right to live and enjoy yourself, was if *all* the significant
people in your life, including your father, indicated 'Yes, dear we
love you immensely, and we think that you are great!'"

"You're quite right," the troubled therapist replied, as she
stopped her crying and began to listen to what the members of the
group were telling her. "I couldn't even stand it, when I was young,
if any of my girlfriends disliked me for any little thing I did. I
thought I *had* to be approved by them. And when I thought they
disliked me, I hated myself."

"Yes," said another group member (who had thus far himself
been defensive about bringing up his problems). "I know what you
mean. I felt exactly the same way when I was a teen-ager. If one of
my friends, or a parent or a relative, showed me that I was expressing myself badly or was acting impolitely, I either thought that they
were accusing me terribly unjustly — or that they were right and I
was an awful person! And I see, the way I am acting here today, that
I still largely have this crazy view. Like you, I measure myself
almost completely by the ratings that others make — or that I *think*
they make — of me. I really think I'm a jerk if they don't think I'm
the greatest thing that ever lived."

"I now see what you mean by my *philosophy*," said the troubled
therapist. "I strongly believe that I cannot accept myself unless
others first accept me — that I don't deserve to enjoy life unless
they think I deserve to enjoy it."

"Right!" said the leader. "You have one of the main irrational
ideas that create so much loneliness and self-deprecation in so

ιny millions of humans: namely, that you don't merely *want* or *refer* significant others to like your actions and prefer to be with you but that you absolutely, utterly *need* their acceptance in order to accept yourself. Now what can you do about minimizing this dire need and changing it back into a desire or preference?"

"Examine it, I guess. Ask myself *why* I cannot do what I want to do, or think I want to do, unless I have the approval of others."

"You're darn right you can examine it!" said still another group member, who up to this time had been strenuously objecting to much of the rational-emotive analysis that had been occurring during the weekend and who had only wanted to go on having individual and group experiences. "And unless you do examine it and examine it, until you decide to give up this asinine philosophy, you'll continue to suffer from its results forever — as you have been doing right now, with us."

"Yes," said the leader. "Now let us see what kind of an activity assignment we can give you to help you combat your I-must-have-love-or-else-I-am-a-slob philosophy."

One of the group members suggested that this therapist, whenever she thereafter spoke up about others' problems in the marathon, also overtly and orally relate them to her own problems and to her own philosophies that lay behind her problems. She accepted this assignment, and carried it out for the rest of the weekend, and reported at the end that she was automatically beginning to see her philosophies much more clearly and to see how she could fight them and change them.[1]

. . . .

Lehman (1973) lists the goals of RET groups while citing their problem-solving nature: (a) bringing to *awareness* problem areas, (b) developing challenges or *attacks* on the problem, (c) devising methods of bringing ideas or plans to *attention,* (d) providing opportunities and plans for *action,* and (e) engaging in *assessment.* Many exercises may be utilized to bring about the awareness of irrational beliefs and illogical emotions. Morris and Cinnamon (1974 a,b), list numerous activities which could be incorporated into a RET approach that uncover problem areas. Procedures to attain the goals of awareness, attack, attention, action, and assessment, may include any of the techniques previously cited by the authors, and any additional innovative ways which effectively assist people to eliminate their irrational fears and accept fallibility in self and others.

[1] *Encounter,* edited by Authur Burton, pp. 117–120, San Francisco: Jossey-Bass, Inc., 1969. Reprinted with permission of the publisher.

McClellan and Stieper (1973) applied the basic principles and concepts of RET using programmed instruction in a structured approach to group marriage counseling. Bibliotherapy was a requirement in conjunction with homework and psychodrama skits related to marital problems. The therapists reported that the group made significant improvements emotionally while gaining a greater capacity for positive communication regarding their problems. This experimental group membership suffered from lengthy marital discord and some members were initially evaluated as psychiatrically disturbed. The research group was conducted in a Veterans Administration outpatient psychiatric clinic and the RET procedure was a new approach for patients considered to be chronically disturbed psychotics and neurotics. Future research on the temporary and long-range results of RET group procedures will provide more baseline data regarding the effectiveness of marathons and experimental groups. Certainly, it can be said that RET procedures in groups will do away with the inefficient use of time, and the lack of verbal interaction so prevalent in the more non-directive approaches. More succinctly, in the RET group, a person who does not verbalize will be made aware of the irrational beliefs preventing such verbalization, dispute such self-talk, and assess the benefits of changing such behavior.

Activities and Applications — Future

The authors see tremendous potential for the use of RET with the elderly. Some of the research underway at the Massachusetts Mental Health Center is very impressive. Shader and Salzman (1974) of the Harvard Medical School have been observing how the elderly handle depression and forgetfulness. This study over the past three years finds a sense of frustration, defeat, and a lack of self-worth causing depression. The researchers find that depression causes the elderly to withdraw into themselves, and that they tend to close themselves off to human interaction. The researchers point out that irritation and forgetfulness experienced by the elderly are commonly thought of as early signs of senility.

The bodily problems with bowels and bladder are said to result from the need for attention, which can be gained by manifesting bodily dysfunction. The amazing thing about the research is that psychotherapy has proven successful for many of the individuals. A reversal of the loss of memory has taken place in many of the elderly. The researchers indicate that group work may eliminate some of the loneliness which brings on depression.

While these approaches and findings are accomplishments of the highest order, as the beginnings of senility do seem to be gone, it is suggested that an RET approach might bring about equal or superior results. When one considers the fact that we live in a culture that highly stresses personal worth and worthlessness — and that the elderly, for the most part, have used their lives to gain value by accepting extrinsic values from the evaluations of others — it is no wonder they find themselves depressed, lonely, and often in some excessive state of self-pity. RET, de-emphasizing external conditions of worth, would lead to self-acceptance. RET principles would indicate philosophically to the elderly that it would be in their best interest to accept their fallibility in the aging process. Our neurosis-encouraging culture subtly directs humans to the retirement status which is construed to mean some ultimate goal or end, while rational-emotive philosophy directs that one who is alive and existing, regardless of age or condition, is actively and presently involved in the *process* of life (limitations of RET stated in Chapter 2 considered).

Educational Input

The implications for future applications of RET principles in education are immense. The in-service training possibilities for faculties and staffs are exciting. The present emphasis upon career education in our schools nearly always includes a decision-making component. Career education is not an *add-on* to the curriculum, nor a K-12 phenomenon, but rather an attempt to modernize education. By noting that it is desirable to consider career education as a life-long process, rational decision-making is imperative from the cradle to the grave. The fact that virtually *all* problem-solving and decision-making capacities involve *intra*personal communication, immediately suggests the use of RET principles.

As Dr. Ellis stated in the interview, the resistance to RET principles in education will probably stem from certain educators' inability to discriminate between emotional education and psychotherapy, plus the possibility that certain educators will cite the imposition of values, etc.

Kanitz: What do you think the resistance is to RET in the schools?

Ellis: Well, we have not really tried that much to get RET into the school system, only in elementary school. I am sure there will be resistance, because first of all some groups will call it psychotherapy instead of emotional education and they will resist on that score. Others will say the same inaccurate thing the Rogerians say, "You are inflicting your values on students."

They don't realize that all therapists, as studies have shown, help change the values of their clients, including the Rogerians.

While these arguments will be forthcoming, one can hardly deny that self-talk precedes every single decision a person makes; similarly, it precedes the solutions to all problems. Much of our self-talk is preconscious rather than conscious, thus the need for a didactic approach to understanding irrational and illogical beliefs. The rational-emotive A-B-C-D-E paradigm is an excellent approach to decision-making and problem-solving, and may easily be adapted to career education components. Since self-awareness is also found in almost every conceptual model for career education, RET and its unique solution to the problem of human worth and self-acceptance has a great deal to offer. The emotional education RET seeks to implement, offers the notion that one does not have to evaluate self, although it is desirable to measure one's abilities objectively.

Teacher education and teachers in general may choose to enter into an RET approach to personal and professional development. By focusing upon attitudes toward students, and feelings and attitudes about self, the individual teacher will gain a greater knowledge about those irrational ideas as manifested in his or her personal behavior. Grieger (1972) lists six irrational attitudes teachers might hold that have a significant impact on the success of consultative efforts to assist teachers as change agents. The attitudes are as follows:

Positive Irrational Attitudes
1. The child needs fixing
2. It is wrong to express negative feelings
3. Children must not be frustrated

Negative Irrational Attitudes
1. The "should-ought" syndrome (that child should behave better, that child ought to behave differently, etc.)
2. The "he/she makes me" syndrome (other people or events cause us to feel the way we do)
3. Children are blameworthy for their misdeeds

The point is made in the article that those educators who maintain these attitudes probably need therapy themselves, and consultation relationships may not be sufficient to bring about improvement. The fact remains that if teachers did examine such irrational beliefs in a rigorously scientific manner, it would eliminate much of the disturbance-proneness manifested by such individuals. Parenthetically, educators disputing their irrational beliefs regarding children will obviously find adults to now be devoid of the wickedness and villainy formerly attributed to them. RET philosophy would be a great boon to contract negotiations between administrators and teachers. The authors contend that if RET principles were the basis for interaction during salary and fringe benefit disputes, a high-level efficient activism would exist, rather than the hostile, anxiety-producing sessions that are so prevalent today in most school districts.

In the interview, Dr. Ellis (1974a) makes some interesting observations regarding future trends. The following presentation is excerpted from the interview.

Ellis: My prediction, and I may be wrong, is that the future trend is in the educational methods. Therapy will be less therapy and more education. Done in big groups, softening-up groups, and via bibliotherapy. Rational-emotive education will also employ TV cassettes as they come along, and other audio-visual aids. So I think that's the future trend. In RET, we are in the vanguard, to a certain degree, because we are a teaching form of therapy, a highly didactic mode. We teach all the time, it is our bailiwick. And we can teach RET principles and practice to individuals, to small groups, and very large groups.

Morris: Do you envision the possibility that you might attempt to build into teacher education programs in New York state and other states RET living principles and theories?

Ellis: Definitely, if they will accept them. Now, to some degree I think they are incorporating emotional education. They often put students of education through encounter groups in teacher education. But if we really show that our stuff works in the school system, I think schools of education will almost automatically adopt some of our methods and make them part of teacher training. Make every teacher, in a sense, an educator-therapist. That would be our goal, since teachers do therapy anyway, and we can specifically train them to do it — as we train our own teachers in our private elementary school, The Living School, in New York City.

Thus, it is the educational model that Ellis predicts will be the future trend. He senses that RET, with its didactic approach, is ready and able to deliver its philosophy and principles to individuals, groups, and institutions desirous of offering emotional education. The authors offer that RET will usually give both individuals and groups philosophic answers to the problems confronting them;

very few problems are catastrophic, and few if any are awful! The future very well could find educational institutions employing RET principles for pure survival reasons.

Concluding Comments

The authors have attempted to present a monograph which portrays a theory of psychotherapy quite different from those illustrated prominently in the professional literature over the past years. RET is not only different, but actually a very radical approach — possibly the most radical since Adler's departure from Freud's classical analytical model. Although many theorists provide excellent baseline data which lends credence to the principles and applications of rational-emotive therapy, it is the prolific writings of Albert Ellis that pinpoint the efficacy of the theory and its practice. The man has virtually developed RET through his own personal growth and development. His private practice has allowed him to deal with thousands of severely disturbed individuals as well as those mildly upset. The successful improvement of a multitude of suffering human beings has proven that reason and emotion are indeed inseparable, and that accepting fallibility in self and others tends to eliminate pernicious condemnation. While the authors do not speak as rational-emotive therapists, it is obvious that RET has many valuable contributions for all persons in the helping professions, i.e., graduated homework, bibliotherapy, the acceptance of all humanity, etc. The more experienced and sophisticated professional, who senses that RET is efficient, will undoubtedly investigate the more involved techniques and creatively apply them.

The authors have found this research to be both rewarding and fulfilling in many ways. We found, in our interview with Dr. Ellis, a very responsive professional, open and congenial to each of us, as well as accepting of those professionals we cited as critical of RET. We have applied certain of the principles and techniques in our personal and professional endeavors, only to find that our writing of this monograph took on an added significance: we were indeed involved in our own bibliotherapy.

We strongly urge the practitioner to consider utilization of some of the RET techniques discussed herein. Graduated homework is, for us, beneficial in introducing *in vivo* change in behavior. Bibliotherapy appears quite useful. The DESIBELS approach has been successfully employed by the authors. These and other techniques can be used by *any* therapist.

APPENDIX

Selected Readings and Resources (Chronologically Ordered)

Ellis, A. & Beechley, R. M. Emotional disturbances in children with peculiar given names. *J. genet. Psychol.*, 1954, 85, 337–339.

———. New approaches to psychotherapy techniques. *J. clin. Psychol.*, 1955, 11, 207–260.(a)

———. Psychotherapy techniques for use with psychotics. *Amer. J. Psychother.*, 1955, 9, 452–476.(b)

———. An operational reformulation of some basic principles of psychoanalysis. *Psychoanal. Rev.*, 1956, 43, 163–180.

———. *How to live with a neurotic.* New York: Crown Publishers, 1957.(a)

———. Outcome of employing three techniques of psychotherapy. *J. clin. Psychol.*, 1957, 13, 344–350.(b)

———. Rational psychotherapy and individual psychology. *J. indiv. Psychol.*, 1957, 13, 38–44.(c)

———. Helping troubled people. *Pastoral Psychol.*, 1958, 9 (82), 33–41.(a)

———. How you can get along with a neurotic. *Today's Living, New York Herald Tribune*, Aug. 3, 1958, 4–5.(b)

———. Hypnotherapy with borderline schizophrenics. *J. gen. Psychol.*, 1958, 59, 245–253.(c)

———. Rational psychotherapy. *J. gen. Psychol.*, 1958, 59, 35–49.(d)

———. The private practice of psychotherapy: a clinical psychologist's report. *J. gen. Psychol.*, 1958, 58, 207–216.(e)

———. A homosexual treated with rational psychotherapy. *J. clin. Psychol.*, 1959, 15, 338–343.(a)

———. Case presentation and several critical comments on the cases of other authors, in S. W. Standal and R. J. Corsini (Eds.), *Critical incidents in psychotherapy*. Englewood Cliffs, N.J.: Prentice-Hall, 1959, pp. 88–91.(b)

———. Psychological aspects of discouraging contraception. *Realist*, 1959, 1 (7), 11–13.(c)

———. Rationalism and its therapeutic applications. *Ann. Psychother.*, 1959, 1 (2), 55–64.(d)

———. Requisite conditions for basic personality change. *J. consult. Psychol.*, 1959, 23, 538–540.(e)

———. *The place of value in the practice of psychotherapy*. New York: American Academy of Psychotherapists, 1959, Annals of Psychotherapy Monograph, No. 2.(f)

———. (Ed.). *What is psychotherapy?* New York: American Academy of Psychotherapists, 1959, Annals of Psychotherapy Monograph, No. 1.(g)

———. What is psychotherapy? — varied approaches to the problem. New York: American Academy of Psychotherapists, 1959, Annals of Psychotherapy Monograph, No. 1, 5–8.(h)

———, Krassner, P., & Wilson, R. A. An impolite interview with Dr. Albert Ellis. *Realist*, 1960, 16, (1), 9–14.(a)

———. Research in psychotherapy. *Newsletter of Psychologists in Private Practice*, Feb., 1960, 1, No. 1, 2.(b)

———. There is no place for the concept of sin in psychotherapy. *J. counsel. Psychol.*, 1960, 7, 188–192.(c)

———, & Harper, R. A. *A guide to rational living in an irrational world*. Englewood Cliffs, N.J.: Prentice-Hall, 1961.(a)

———. A rational approach to premarital counseling. *Psychol. Rep.*, 1961, 8, 333–338.(b)

———, & Harper, R. A. *Creative marriage*. New York: Lyle Stuart, 1961.(c)

———. On Reiss and Durkin on Ellis on Fried on Freud. *Contemp. Psychol.*, 1961, 6, 382.(d)

———. Rational therapy applied. *Balanced Living*, Oct., 1961, 17, 292–296.(e)

———. Treatment of a psychopath with rational psychotherapy. *J. Psychol.*, 1961, 51, 141–150.(f)

———. Morality and therapy. *Columbia University Forum*, Spring, 1962, 6, No. 2, 47–48.(a)

———. *Reason and emotion in psychotherapy*. New York: Lyle Stuart, 1962.(b)

———. *The American sexual tragedy*. (2nd. ed.) New York: Lyle Stuart, 1962.(c)

———. *Rational-emotive psychotherapy*. New York: Institute for Rational Living, 1963.(a)

———. Rational-emotive psychotherapy: a critique of three critiques. *Bull.*

Essex County Soc. Clin. Psychologists in Private Practice, Spring, 1963, 6–10.(b)

———, & Wolf, R. An interview with Dr. Albert Ellis. *Campus Voice,* 1964, Issue 19, 6–11.(a)

———, Averitt, C., & Lipton, L. A talk with Dr. Ellis. *Los Angeles Free Press,* Sept. 10, 1964, 3.(b)

———. Thoughts on theory versus outcome in psychotherapy. *Psychother.: Theor., Res., Prac.,* 1964, 1 (2), 83–87.(c)

———. An answer to some objections to rational-emotive psychotherapy. *Psychother.: Theor., Res., Prac.,* 1965, 2 (3), 108–111.(a)

———. Showing the patient that he is not a worthless individual. *Voices,* 1965, 1 (2), 74–77.(b)

———. *The case for sexual liberty: I.* Tucson: Seymour Press, 1965.(c)

———. The treatment of psychotic and borderline psychotic patients with rational-emotive psychotherapy, in *Symposium on therapeutic methods with schizophrenics.* Battle Creek, Mich.: Veterans Administration Hospital, 1965. pp. 5–32.(d)

———. The use of printed, written and recorded words in psychotherapy, in L. Pearson, (Ed.) *The use of written communications in psychotherapy.* Springfield, Ill.: Charles C. Thomas, 1965. pp. 23–36.(e)

———. Bibliotherapy: books on marriage for clients. *Voices,* 1966, 2, 83–85.(a)

———. Continuing personal growth of the psychotherapist: a rational-emotive view. *J. human. Psychol.,* 1966, 6 (2), 156–169.(b)

———, Wolfe, Janet, & Moseley, Sandra. *How to prevent your child from becoming a neurotic adult.* New York: Crown Publishers, 1966.(c)

———. Should non-professionals be trained to do psychotherapy? *Newsletter, Division of Clinical Psychology of the APA,* Spring, 1966, 19 (2), 10–11.(d)

———. The nature of disturbed marital interaction. *Rational Living,* 1966, 1 (1), 22–26.(e)

———. Goals of psychotherapy, in A. R. Mahrer (Ed.), *The goals of psychotherapy.* New York: Appleton-Century-Crofts, 1967, pp. 206–220.(a)

———. Objectivism, the new religion. *Rational Living,* 1967, 2 (2), 1–6.(b)

———. Phobia treated with rational-emotive psychotherapy. *Voices,* 1967, 3 (3), 34–40.(c)

———. Rational-emotive psychotherapy, in D. S. Arbuckle (Ed.), *Counseling and psychotherapy.* New York: McGraw-Hill, 1967, pp. 78–106.(d)

———, & Blum, M. L. Rational training: a new method of facilitating management and labor relations. *Psychol. Rep.,* 1967, 20 (3), Pt. II, 1267–1284.(e)

———. Reason and emotion in psychotherapy. *Pop. Psychol.,* May, 1967, 1 (1), 30–32, 59–62.(f)

————.Self acceptance and successful human relations. *Newsletter of the Inst. for Marriage and Friendship and Sci. Introduction Center,* Winter 1967, 3, 8–9.(g)

————. Should some people be labeled mentally ill? *J. Consult. Psychol.,* 1967, 31 (5), 435–446.(h)

————. Talking to adolescents about sex. *Rational Living,* 1967, 2 (1), 7–12.(i)

————. A rational approach to interpretation, in E. F. Hammer (Ed.), *Use of interpretation in treatment.* New York: Grune and Stratton, 1968.(a)

————. Healthy and disturbed reasons for having extra-marital relations. *J. hum. Relat.,* 1968, 16 (4), 490–501.(b)

————. Is psychoanalysis harmful? *Psychiat. Opin.,* 1968, 5 (1), 16–24.(c)

————. Objectivism, the new religion: II. *Rational Living,* 1968, 3 (1), 12–19.(d)

————. What really causes psychotherapeutic change? *Voices,* 1968, 4 (2), 90–97.(e)

————. A cognitive approach to behavior therapy. *Int. J. Psychiat.,* 1969, 8, 896–900.(a)

————. A critical evaluation of marriage counseling, in B. N. Ard Jr. & C. C. Ard (Eds.), *Handbook of marriage counseling.* Palo Alto: Science and Behavior Books, 1969.(b)

————. A rational approach to premarital counseling, in B. N. Ard Jr. & C. C. Ard (Eds.), *Handbook of marriage counseling.* Palo Alto: Science and Behavior Books, 1969.(c)

————. A weekend of rational encounter, in A. Burton (Ed.), *Encounter.* San Francisco: Jossey-Bass, 1969, pp. 112–127.(d)

————. Comments on C. H. Patterson, "Current view of client-centered or relationship therapy." *Counseling Psychol.,* 1969, 1 (2), 37–42.(e)

————. Emotional problems of the young adult. In Forest Hospital Foundation (Ed.), *The young adult.* Des Plaines, Ill.: Forest Hosp. Foundation, 1969, pp. 83–102.(f)

————. How to increase sexual enjoyment in marriage, in B. N. Ard & C. C. Ard (Eds.), *Handbook of marriage counseling.* Palo Alto: Science and Behavior Books, 1969.(g)

————. & Havelock Ellis, in D. Sills (Ed.) *International encyclopedia of the social sciences.* New York: Macmillan, 1969.(h)

————, & Elliott, J. Irrational ideas. *Explorations,* Winter 1969–70, 17, 13–16.(i)

————. Neurotic interaction between marital partners, in B. N. Ard Jr. & C. C. Ard (Eds.), *Handbook of marriage counseling.* Palo Alto: Science and Behavior Books, 1969.(j)

————. Rational emotive therapy. *J. contemp. Psychother.,* 1969, 1 (2), 82–90.(k)

————. Rational-emotive therapy in the private practice of psychotherapy. *J. contemp. Psychother.,* 1969, 1, 82–94.(1)

————. Rationality in sexual morality. *The Humanist,* 1969, 29 (5), 17–21.(m)

————. Teaching emotional education in the classroom. *School Health Rev.,* November, 1969, 10–13.(n)

————. *The essence of rational psychotherapy: a comprehensive approach to treatment.* New York: Inst. for Advanced Study in Rational Psychotherapy, 1969.(o)

————. Where can we go from here? *Psychology Today,* Jan., 1969, 2 (8), 38.(p)

————. A weekend of rational encounter. *Rational Living,* 1970, 4 (2), 1–8.(a)

————. Humanism, values, rationality, in Tributes to Alfred Adler on his 100th birthday. *J. indl. Psychol.,* May, 1970, 26, 11–12.(b)

————. Rational-emotive therapy, in L. Hersher (Ed.), *Four Psychotherapies.* New York: Appleton-Century-Crofts, 1970.(c)

————. The cognitive element in experiential and relationship psychotherapy. *Existential Psychiatry,* 1970, 7 (28), 35–52.(d)

————. The emerging counselor. *Canadian Counselor,* 1970, 4 (2), 99–105.(e)

————. *The essence of rational psychotherapy: a comprehensive approach to treatment.* New York: Institute for Rational Living, 1970.(f)

————, & Casriel, D. Debate: Albert Ellis vs. Daniel Casriel on anger. *Rational Living,* 1971, 6 (2), 2–21.(a)

————. An experiment in emotional education. *Educ. Technol.,* 1971, 11 (7), 61–64.(b)

————. *Growth through reason.* Palo Alto: Science and Behavior Books, 1971.(c)

————, & Gullo, J. M. *Murder and assassination.* New York: Lyle Stuart, 1971.(d)

————, & Lehman, Patricia. Practical applications of rational-emotive technique. *Rational Living,* 1971, 6 (2), 36–38.(e)

————. Problems of daily living workshop, in R. J. Menges and F. Pennington (Eds.), *A survey of nineteen innovative educational programs for adolescents and adults.* Minneapolis: Youth Research Center, 1971, pp. 49–51.(f)

————. Psychotherapy and the value of a human being, in Davis, J. W. (Ed.), *Value and valuation: essays in honor of Robert S. Hartman.* Knoxville: University of Tennessee Press, 1971.(g)

————. *Rational-emotive therapy and its application to emotional education.* New York: Institute for Rational Living, 1971.(h)

————. Reason and emotion in the individual psychology of Adler. *J. indiv. Psychol.,* 1971, 27 (1), 50–64.(i)

————. Sexual problems of the young adult. *Rational Living,* 1971, 5 (2), 1–11.(j)

————. 22 ways to stop putting yourself down. *Rational Living*, 1971, 6 (1), 8–15.(k)

————. Emotional education in the classroom: the Living school. *J. clin. child Psychol.*, 1972, 1 (3), 19–22.(a)

————. *Executive leadership: a rational approach.* New York: Citadel Press, 1972.(b)

————. Helping people get better rather than merely feel better. *Rational Living*, 1972, 7 (2), 2–9.(c)

————. Humanistic psychotherapy: a revolutionary approach. *The Humanist*, 1972, 32 (1), 24–28.(d)

————, & Lehman, Patricia. New developments and techniques in RET. *Rational Living*, 1972, 7 (1), 34–35, 40.(e)

————. Philosophy and rational emotive therapy. *Counsel. Values*, 1972, 16 (3), 158–161.(f)

————. Rational-emotive psychotherapy: a comprehensive approach to therapy, in G. D. Goldman & D. S. Milman (Eds.), *Innovations in psychotherapy.* Springfield, Ill.: Charles C. Thomas, 1972.(g)

————. *Suggested procedures for a weekend of rational encounter,* (2nd ed.). New York: Institute for Advanced Study in Rational Psychotherapy, 1972.(h)

————. The contribution of psychotherapy to school psychology. *School Psychol. Dig.*, 1972, 1 (2), 6–9.(i)

————. Emotional education at the Living School, in M. M. Ohlsen (Ed.), *Counseling children in groups.* New York: Holt, Rinehart, and Winston, 1973, pp. 79–93.(a)

————. Healthy and unhealthy aggression. Paper presented at the American Psychological Association 81st Annual Convention, Montreal, August 27, 1973.(b)

————. *Humanistic psychotherapy.* New York: Julian Press, 1973.(c)

————. Rational-emotive psychotherapy, in R. Corsini (Ed.), *Contemporary psychotherapies.* Itasca, Ill.: Peacock, 1973.(d)

————. Rational-emotive psychotherapy, in R. M. Jurjevich (Ed.), *Direct Psychotherapies.* Miami: University of Miami Press, 1973, pp. 295–327.(e)

————. The no cop-out therapy. *Psychology Today*, 1973, 7 (2), 56–62.(f)

————. Interview with authors. Conducted at Rational-emotive therapy workshop, Western Illinois University, Macomb, February, 1974.(a)

————. Rational-emotive therapy workshop. Presented at Western Illinois University, Macomb, February, 1974.(b)

BIBLIOGRAPHY

Arbuckle, D. S. *Counseling and psychotherapy: an overview.* New York: McGraw Hill, 1967.

Ard, B. N., Jr. The A-B-C of marriage counseling. *Rational Living,* 1967, 2(2), 10–12.

———. Rational therapy in rehabilitation counseling. *Rehabilit. counsel. Bull.,* 1968, 12, 84–88.

Ard, B. N. A rational approach to marriage counseling, in Ard, B. N., Jr. & Ard, C. C. (Eds.), *Handbook of marriage counseling.* Palo Alto: Science and Behavior Books, 1969. pp. 115–119.

Beck, A. T. Cognitive therapy: nature and relation to behavior therapy. *Behav. Ther.,* 1970, 1, 184–200.

———, & Hurvich, M. S. Psychological correlates of depression. *Psychosom. Med.,* 1959, 21, 50–55.

———, & Stein, D. The self concept in depression. Unpublished study summarized in Beck, A. T. *Depression: clinical, experimental and theoretical aspects.* New York: Hoeber-Harper, 1967.

Becker, J. Achievement-related characteristics of manic-depressives. *J. abnorm. soc. Psychol.,* 1960, 60 334–339.

———, Spielberger, C. D., & Parker, J. B. Value achievement and authoritarian attitudes in psychiatric patients. *J. clin. Psychol.,* 1963, ·19, 57–61.

Bednar, R. L. Persuasibility and the power of belief. *Personnel Guid. J.*, 1970, 48, 647–652.

Breen, G. Active-directive counseling in an adult education center. *J. coll. student Personnel*, July 1970, 279–283.

Burton, A. (Ed.). *Encounter.* San Francisco: Jossey-Bass, Inc., 1969.

——, & Associates. *Twelve therapists.* San Francisco: Jossey Bass, Inc., 1972.

Callahan, R. Overcoming religious faith. *Rational Living*, 1967, 2(1), 16–21.

Carlson, W. A., Travers, R. M. W., & Schwab, E. A., Jr. A laboratory approach to the cognitive control of anxiety. Paper read at the American Personnel and Guidance Association Meetings, March 31, 1969.

Cavior, U., & Cone, J. D. The adult irrational ideas inventory: its factor structure and correlations with measures of social desirability. *Proceedings of the Annual Convention of the American Psychological Association*, 1972, 7, Pt. I.

Cooke, G. The efficacy of two desensitization procedures: an analogue study. *Behav. Res. & Ther.*, 1966, 4, 17–24.

Davies, R. L. Relationship of irrational ideas to emotional disturbance. M.Ed. thesis, University of Alberta, 1970.

Davison, G. C. Relative contributions of differential relaxation and graded exposure to in vivo desensitization of a neurotic fear. *Proceedings of the 72nd Annual Convention of the American Psychological Association*, 1965, pp. 209–210.

——. Anxiety under total curarization: implications for the role of muscular relaxation in the desensitization of neurotic fears. *J. neru. ment. Dis.*, 1967, 143, 443–448.

——, & Valins, S. Maintainence of self-attributed and drug attributed behavior change. *J. pers. soc. Psychol.*, 1969, 11, 25–33.

Deane, G. E. Human heart rate responses during experimentally induced anxiety: effects of instruction on acquisition. *J. exp. Psychol.*, 1966, 67 193–195.

Diamond, L. Restoring amputated ego. *Rational Living*, 1967, 2 (2), 15.

di Loreto, A. A comparison of the relative effectiveness of systematic desensitization, rational-emotive, and client-centered group psychotherapy in the reduction of interpersonal anxiety in introverts and extroverts. Doctoral dissertation, Michigan State University, 1969.

——. *Comparative Psychotherapy.* Chicago: Aldine-Atherton Inc., 1971.

Dua, P. S. Comparison of the effects of behaviorally oriented action and psychotherapy reeducation on introversion, extroversion, emotionality, and internal-external control. *J. counsel. Psychol.*, 1970, 17, 567–572.

Education Research Group. The law of mental declension. *J. Inst. comp. Study Hist., Philo., Sci.*, 1967, 5 (3), 233–234.

Epictetus. *The works of Epictetus.* Boston: Little Brown, 1899.

Fox, E. E. & Davis, R. L. Test your rationality. *Rational Living,* 1971, 5 (2), 23–25.

Frank, J. The influence of patients' and therapists' expectations on the outcome of psychotherapy. *British J. med. Psychol.,* 1968, 41, 349–356.

Garfield, Z. H., Darwin, P. L., Singer, B. A., & McBrearty, J. F. Effect of "in vivo" training on experimental desensitization of a phobia. *Psychol. Rep.,* 1967, 20, 215–219.

Glass, D. D., Singer, J. E., & Freidman, L. N. Psychic cost of adaptation to environment stressor. *J. pers. soc. Psychol.,* 1969, 12, 200–210.

Glicken, M. D. Counseling children. *Rational Living,* 1966, 1(2), 27–30.

———. A rational approach to short term counseling. *J. psychiat. Nurs. ment. hlth Serv.,* 1968, 6(6), 336–338.

Grieger, R. Teacher attitudes as a variable in behavior modification. *Rational Living,* 1972, 7(2), 14–19.

Grossack, M. *You are not alone.* Boston: Christopher Publishing House, 1965.

Gullo, J. M. Counseling hospital patients. *Rational Living,* 1966, 1(2), 11–15.(a)

———. Useful variations on RET. *Rational Living,* 1966, 1(1), 44–45.(b)

Harper, R. A. *Psychoanalysis and psychotherapy: thirty-six systems.* Englewood Cliffs, New Jersey: Prentice-Hall, Inc., 1959.

Hauck, P. The neurotic agreement in psychotherapy. *Rational Living,* 1966, 1(1), 31–34.

———. Challenge authority-for thy health's sake. *Rational Living,* 1967, 2(1), 1–3.

———. An open letter to us. *Rational Living,* 1968, 3(1), 29–30.

Jones, R. G. A factorial measure of Ellis' irrational belief system with personality and maladjustment correlates. Doctoral thesis, Texas Technological College, 1968.

Jourard, S. *Disclosing man to himself.* Princeton: Van Nostrand, 1968.

Jurjevich, R. M. *Direct psychotherapy.* Coral Gables, Florida: University of Miami Press, 1973.

Karst, T. O. & Trexler, L. D. Initial study using fixed-role and rational-emotive therapy in treating public-speaking anxiety. *J. consult, Psychol.,* 1970, 34, 360–366.

Kempel, L. T. Identifying and confronting ways of prematurely terminating therapy. *Rational Living,* 1973, 8 (1), 6–9.

Kierkegaard, S. *Philosophical fragments.* New Jersey: Princeton University Press, 1962.

Knaus, W. J. Overcoming procrastination. *Rational Living,* 1973, 8 (2), 2–7.

Lang, P. J., Sroufe, L. A., & Hastings, J. E. Effects of feedback and instructional set on the control of cardiac variability. *J. exp. Psychol.,* 1967, 75, 425–431.

Laughridge, S. An approach to handling resistance to interpretation. *Rational Living*, 1972, 7 (2), 29–31.

Lehman, Patricia. Practical applications of RET: group techniques. *Rational Living*, 1973, 8 (1), 32–36.

Litvak, S. B. A comparison of two brief group behavior therapy techniques on the reduction of avoidance behavior. *Psychol. Rec.*, 1969, 19, 329–334.

Maslow, A. H. *The farther reaches of human nature.* New York: Viking Press, 1971.

Maultsby, M. C., Jr. The pamphlet as a therapeutic aid. *Rational Living*, 1968, 3 (2), 31–35.

Maultsby, M. C. Routine tape recorder use in RET. *Rational Living*, 1970, 5 (1), 8–23.

———. Rational-emotive imagery. *Rational Living*, 1971, 6 (1), 16–23.(a)

———. Systematic, written homework in psychotherapy. *Psychotherapy*, 1971, 8 (3), 195–198.(b)

May, R. *Love and will.* New York: Norton, 1969.

McClellan, T. & Stieper, D. A structural approach to group marriage counseling. *Rational Living*, 1973, 8 (2), 12–18.

Meichenbaum, D. Ways of modifying what clients say to themselves. *Ontario Psychologist*, 1972, 4 (3), 144–151.

Mitscheslich, A. Rationale therapie and psychotherapie. (Rational therapy and psychotherapy.) *Psyche. Heidel.*, 1958, 12, 721–731.

Morris, K. & Cinnamon, K. *Handbook of nonverbal group exercises.* Springfield, Ill.: Charles C. Thomas, 1974.(a)

———. *Handbook of verbal group exercises.* Springfield, Ill.: Charles C. Thomas, 1974.(b)

Nisbett, R. E. & Schacter, S. Cognitive manipulation of pain. *J. exp. soc. Psychol.*, 1966, 2, 227–236.

Patterson, C. H. *Theories of counseling and psychotherapy.* New York: Harper and Row, 1966.

Rand, M. E. Rational-emotive approach to academic underachievement. *Rational Living*, 1970, 4 (2), 16–18.

Rimm, D. C. & Litvak, S. B. Self-verbalization and emotional arousal. *J. abnorm. Psychol.*, 1969, 74, 181–187.

Ritter, B. The group desensitization of childrens' snake phobias using vicarious and contact desensitization procedures. *Behav. res. Ther.*, 1968, 6, 1–6.

Schacter, S. & Singer, J. R. Cognitive, social, and physiological determinants of emotional state. *Psychol. Rev.*, 1962, 69, 379–399.

Sherman, S. Alcoholism and group therapy. *Rational Living*, 1967, 2 (2), 20–22.

Taft, G. L. A study of the relationship of anxiety and irrational ideas. Doctoral dissertation, University of Alberta. 1965.

Tosi, D. J. *Youth: toward personal growth.* Columbus: Charles E. Merrill, 1974.

Trexler, L. D. & Karst, T. O. Rational-emotive therapy, placebo, and no-treatment effects on public speaking anxiety. *J. abnorm. Psychol.*, 1972, 79 (1), 60–67.

Trexler, L. D. The suicidal person and the restoration of hope. *Rational Living*, 1973, 8 (2), 19–23.

Valins, S. Cognitive effects of false heart-rate feedback. *J. pers. soc. Psychol.*, 1966, 4, 400–408.

———— & Ray, A. A. Effects of cognitive desensitization on avoidance behavior. *J. pers. soc. Psychol.*, 1967, 7, 345–350.

Vertis, R. The rational emotion: a definition. *Rational Living*, 1970, 4 (2), 19–20.

Winsten, J. A. A way to reverse memory loss. *The Detroit Free Press*, February 24, 1974.

Wolberg, L. R. *The technique of psychotherapy.* New York: Grune and Stratton, 1967.

Wolfe, Janet, et. al. Emotional education in the classroom: the living school. *Rational Living*, 1970, 4 (2), 22–25.

Zajonc, R. B. Attitudinal effects of mere exposure. *J. pers. soc. Psychol.*, 1968, 9 (Part II, Monograph Supplement).

Zingle, H. W. A rational therapy approach to counseling under-achievers. Doctoral dissertation, University of Alberta, 1965.

INDEX